EMPATHY SELLING

Christopher C. Golis MA, MSc, FSIA is a Cambridge and London Business School graduate who began his sales career in 1974 with ICL. There, in his first year on quota, he sold $1.4 million and took the only account from IBM for ICL worldwide. For four years he was General Manager of the TNT Payroll Management Systems Division where he trained the sales staff in Empathy Selling techniques. They doubled volumes, quadrupled revenues and took the annual profit from $100,000 to over $1 million.

Chris Golis joined the merchant bank, BT Australia Limited, in 1981 to start the Financial Services Division and launched the BT High Yield and BT Split Trust which now, between them, exceed $1 billion in assets.

He currently works in the venture capital industry and is a director of Scitec Communications Systems Ltd, DKS Pty Ltd, Neverfail Springwater Pty Ltd and Quantum Technology Pty Ltd.

For Chris Golis, selling is the toughest job of all. He is 'outnumbered' at his Sydney home by a wife and two daughters.

There are times when I look over the various parts of my character with perplexity. I recognise that I am made up of several persons and that the person that at the moment has the upper hand will inevitably give place to another. But which is the real one? All of them or none?

W. Somerset Maugham

EMPATHY SELLING

THE POWERFUL NEW SALES TECHNIQUE FOR THE 1990s

Christopher C Golis

KOGAN
PAGE

First published in 1991 in Australia
by Lothian Publishing Company Pty Ltd
11 Munro Street, Port Melbourne, Victoria 3207

This edition published in 1992 in the UK
by the undermentioned

Kogan Page Limited
120 Pentonville Road
London N1 9JN

British Library Cataloguing in Publication Data

A CIP record for this book is available from the British Library.

ISBN 0 7494 0888 X

Printed in England by Clays Ltd, St Ives plc

CONTENTS

Acknowledgements

Many people helped me to edit and revise this book. Among them Juliana Robertson, Nick Forrester and Hugh Wallace are some of the very few natural salespeople I have met. All are superb at developing empathy with a client. Nevertheless, all would agree that if a rival diligently applied the techniques described in this book then they would have to work hard to compete successfully.

I would like to thank Samantha Osborne and Suzanne Halliday, who typed the first manuscript, and Suzette Simpson, Jan Proudfoot, Peter Abelson, Dr Blair Stone, Toni Grunseit and Graeme Nicholls for their help in editing the manuscripts. Finally I would especially like to thank Jill Hickson who, besides making a number of useful contributions, provided the final shove up the mountain.

PREFACE

All books on selling, like all salespeople, should have an objective. The objective of *Empathy Selling* is simple. It is to describe a method of helping you to close more sales more quickly by understanding your clients better. Empathy is the ability to grasp or understand another person's point of view. *Empathy Selling*, uniquely, describes how to develop empathy by discovering your prospect's hidden but dominant desires.

For over fifteen years I have pursued the career of selling; I worked as a salesperson; I have trained salespeople; I have managed salespeople. One lesson that I learned in the first month is as true now as it was then; selling is an emotional process. After a sale much will be said about the logical reasons for purchasing a product or service. All good salespeople know that these post-decision justifications are superfluous — the sale occurs at that moment when the decision-maker suddenly desires your product. The purpose of this book is to help you uncover the diverse desires of different buyers and tailor your sales technique accordingly.

It is people who buy — and people are emotional. People have likes and dislikes. People have desires. Understand and apply the lessons in this book and you cannot fail to improve both your financial rewards and your personal satisfaction from selling.

Successful selling requires several skills. Winning salespeople must have and know how to generate a positive mental attitude. They require thorough knowledge of their products and their competition. Professional salespeople also need to learn the various sales techniques such as telephoning for interviews, territory organisation and handling objections. There are many books and courses about these topics.

Empathy Selling, on the other hand, is new and different. It teaches you how to analyse your prospects and establish their dominant desires, using various clues such as the way they talk and dress. You gain empathy with your prospect and learn how to vary your sales presentations. No longer will you just close sales — you will learn how to open relationships.

Empathy Selling is systematic. It distinguishes many personality types, is easy to learn because of a basic principle of human behaviour and, most important of all, is both fun and profitable to use. Everyone who has invested the two or three days that are needed to master the method has become a firm believer in and a user of the system.

The question has been raised whether salespeople are born or made. There is a certain personality which makes for a 'natural' salesperson. In the same way that a chameleon can match its skin colouring to the physical environment, natural salespeople can instinctively adapt their personalities to those of individual buyers.

Instinct is not infallible and the professional salesperson will prefer to use a technique that leaves little to chance. The techniques that you will learn in this book will put a powerful set of people-handling tools in your kit bag.

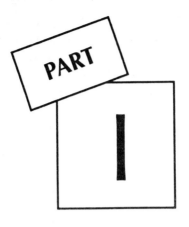

PART

1

WHAT IS
EMPATHY
SELLING?

*I*NTRODUCTION

ANYONE who has sold soon recognises that during a successful sale a moment comes when the prospect suddenly becomes emotionally committed to the product. This moment is sometimes called 'hooking the customer' or 'hitting the hot button'. All good salespeople know that, even when you give a technically perfect presentation and try hundreds of closes, no sale will be made unless emotional commitment is obtained from the customer.

This key to selling is well recognised. Nearly all books on selling have a section devoted to empathy. Empathy is defined as projecting your personality inside the minds of your prospects and trying to understand their viewpoints. Yet, while everyone agrees on the importance of empathy, little advice is given on how to achieve it with a prospect. The advice usually consists of simple catchphrases such as 'ask questions' or 'listen, listen, listen'.

The purpose of this book is to help you better understand how people tick. By developing a better understanding of yourself and other people you should be able to develop better customer relationships. Moreover, if the emotional climate is harmonious you have a better chance of developing a consultative role with your client. It has long been understood that the truly successful salespeople are those regarded as independent mentors by their clients.

Before the introduction of electronic-media mass marketing, particularly television, the door-to-door salesperson was a familiar sight. Unfortunately the sales profession developed a shoddy image and a lack of professional qualifications helped to debase the career. Furthermore, the increasing use of advertising to presell goods meant that sales executives were downgraded into order-takers and inventory-checkers.

This state of affairs is now changing. Industrial products have become much more complex and the investment in their marketing is considerable. Computer sales executives for a major competitive corporate sale, for example, will be managing up to a dozen people for two years. Furthermore the growth of the services sector, which now represents as much as 70 per cent of many developed economies, has meant that many professional and neoprofessional organisations have had either to employ new sales staff or to train their existing staff in sales techniques. The concentration of the retail sector and the development of central buying committees has also meant that the people selling or servicing those committees have had to develop improved sales skills. Finally, the far higher general standards of education have led to the rise of consumerism, which means that the client's sense of awe has disappeared — people will no longer be impressed by the foot-in-the-door, fast-talking techniques of the snake-oil salesman.

To sell you must have someone who is willing to buy. Buying can be refined into three fundamentally distinct situations:

1 The *New Task* when a product is being purchased for the first time.
2 The *Modified Rebuy* when a change in product or supplier is taking place.
3 The *Routine Rebuy* when there are regular purchases of the same product.

New-Task purchasing is nearly always competitive. In both the industrial and consumer durable market buyers usually begin by seeking information. Just reflect on your last major purchase of a new product for the home, such as a VCR or compact disc player. Typically you will have done some research, collected information and visited several shops or had meetings with sales representatives. Competitive pressure generally results in most products being of similar price, quality and specifications. What is the difference and what product did you finally choose? Generally the one sold by the salesperson whom you (or your spouse) thought you could trust.

The same process occurs in the industrial world. As a result of product research and development, production engineering, a change in management or a consultant's report, an organisation decides to buy a product or service. On most occasions there is a search for competitive suppliers. While the decision will ultimately be rationalised on the grounds of price, delivery schedules, better commercial reputation and so on, the decision will generally be based on the sales representative who is first to discover the decision-making structure of the company, develops empathy with the decision-makers and influencers, and finds out what the customer needs and wants.

The next type of purchase is the Modified Rebuy, when a buyer is considering a change of product or supplier. This can happen for a variety of reasons, such as an increase in price or poor delivery by the incumbent or creative marketing by a potential supplier. In either case Empathy Selling plays a critical role. The sales representative must re-establish credibility for the incumbent supplier. In order to do that the salesperson needs to have empathy with the buyer. Often the answer is no because either the buyer or the sales representative is new to the job or territory. Then it becomes a race between the incumbent salesperson and the competition to develop better empathy with the buyer. If the salesperson is new and the competition has been calling on the client for some considerable time and has launched a new product or commercial policy, the task can be quite difficult. A key to success is understanding the buyer and here Empathy Selling can be very useful.

For the outside salesperson looking to gain new business from a prospect who is buying from a competitor, Empathy Selling is critical. Often the salesperson will only have one bite at the cherry and must create a favourable impression if he or she is to get to explain the company's products or services. If the non-incumbent salesperson cannot rapidly generate empathy with the new prospect, all the hard work of breaking into the account will be wasted.

The Routine Rebuy is another situation in which Empathy Selling plays a crucial role. All of us have favourite shops where we repeatedly go to make habitual purchases. A family will typically have several favourite restaurants where it will regularly spend some of its disposable income. People tend over time to choose those shops and services where they feel most comfortable and perceive the staff as being pleasant and understanding.

The same applies to industrial markets. Typically, an industrial buyer will have several alternative suppliers of routine repurchases listed in the company internal reorder procedures. The buying company policy will usually be to mix up the orders so as to maintain sources of alternative supply. The key to winning orders is a knowledge of what the competition is doing, particularly in pricing. If the sales representative has developed good empathy with the buyer, such information will be more readily available. Furthermore, the skill of the salesperson lies in getting more than the 'fair' market share. If a salesperson can get say 40 per cent of the annual orders from a client while the other two competitors get, say, 30 per cent each, the difference to the salesperson's company will be significant. It may not merely be that the level of orders will be one-third higher; the extra loading on the factory may mean that the job is done at near full capacity and therefore at lower average cost per unit, so that more profits will result.

In summary, we have now demonstrated why developing an understanding of clients is important. First it helps you to gain emotional commitment from a prospect. Second, as selling is now much more complex, understanding clients is a key to developing the necessary sensitivity for success. Finally, in all three basic buying situations there is competition, and Empathy Selling can provide the competitive edge.

*T*HE SEVEN BASIC DESIRES

HY do people buy? This has been the subject of much research by many organisations and people. Generally most agree that people buy a product or service for themselves or their organisations not because of some combination of features but because of perceived benefits. Those benefits, in turn, satisfy some form of motivational need or desire.

When I first began my selling career, as a computer sales-person, one of the first lessons I was taught was to distinguish between the needs and wants of the organisation. A private-sector organisation needs products and services that increase its profit. These can be products or services which cut operating costs, increase efficiency or increase sales. The wants of an organisation are the desires of its decision-makers.

The first postulate of this book is that there are seven basic desires present in every buyer. The rationale for this belief is described in the final chapter. Every individual has these seven desires to some degree.

The Seven Basic Desires

1 The desire to communicate.
2 The desire for security.
3 The desire to be creative.
4 The desire to win.
5 The desire to complete projects.
6 The desire for material success.
7 The desire for social approval.

The second postulate of this book is that the variation and mix of these desires are reflected in the personality of the individual and that, in every individual, several desires are dominant. The art of Empathy Selling is to learn how to recognise the dominant desires and then tailor your sales strategy accordingly.

If a person had only one excessively dominant desire, his or her personality would deteriorate into a caricature; such people do not exist in real life. Nevertheless, to explain the techniques of Empathy Selling it is convenient to describe hypothetical individuals who are dominated by one desire. We describe these theoretical individuals as stereotypes and ascribe a stereotype name to each desire, as shown in the table below.

The Dominant Desires and Stereotypes

Stereotype	Dominant Desire
Normal	Desire for social approval
Mover	Desire to communicate
Ditherer	Desire for security
Artist	Desire to be creative
Politician	Desire to win
Engineer	Desire to complete projects
Hustler	Desire for material success

When describing someone users of Empathy Selling often just employ the first letter of the stereotype. Thus a person may be described as a 'Little-H', 'Big-P', 'Strong-E', 'Weak-D', 'High-M' or 'Low-N'.

Each of the seven desires is present in all of us and each, at some time or another, affects our personality. As we shall see later there is a whole host of other behaviours related to each desire. Rather than repeatedly using the word desire, which also has emotional connotations, we will also use the term 'component' when speaking about different personality types. Thus we might say that an accountant has a big Normal component.

The following seven chapters discuss each of the personality stereotypes in depth. After an introduction, each chapter has a short imaginary dialogue between a salesperson and prospect of the relevant stereotype. The next section then describes the clues that allow you to identify the prospect's dominant buying desire. Then we discuss how a personality totally obsessed by this desire would behave. In reality, and this cannot be stressed enough, few personalities are completely dominated by one desire. However, it is easier to understand each type by describing a theoretical individual dominated by one desire. In this way the reader should develop empathy with each of the temperament types. To help in understanding, examples are taken from two classic marketing areas — the dominant themes in different decades of advertising and the type of car the theoretical individual would buy.

To provide a contrast, the personality of someone lacking the particular desire is briefly described. These opposite personalities or 'antitypes' are more difficult to detect, but it can be useful to identify them when deciding on a selling strategy.

The next section of the book deals with the various stages of the sale: the approach, presentation, objections and closes. This section shows how a knowledge of personality types is invaluable in developing empathy with your clients and building up relationships with them.

Most people lack the instinct or intuition of the great writers; they assume that other people act and behave just as they themselves do, with only limited variation. Only when sales executives develop empathy with prospects and clients do they begin to understand how diverse people really are.

The Four Ps

When I first began to sell I was taught to remember the 'four Ps' of the successful sales executive: Positive thinking, Persistence, Present benefits and Passion. By passion my mentors meant that sales presentations should contain enthusiasm and emotion. Emotion is an important component of a presentation.

In this book I intend to extend the meaning of 'passion' and show how to understand the various emotions present in a buyer and adapt your sales presentation to the dominant desires.

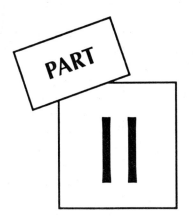

PART

II

THE
SEVEN
STEREOTYPES

*T*HE MOVER

IN the BBC television series *Life on Earth*, David Attenborough described humans as 'the compulsive communicators'. He postulated that the human being's passion to communicate and receive communication was as important to our success as fins were to fish or feathers to birds. This desire to communicate is probably the most basic and common of all desires and that is why the Mover is perhaps the most common dominant desire. In the cameo below we describe the stereotype of a prospect dominated by this one desire.

Movers are often found working in organisations that require a lot of contact with people. Good examples are the fast food, car rental and retail industries.

I currently work in the field of venture capital. I have looked at over 800 business propositions. One product was a toothbrush which was made of a special type of thermoplastic which would bend under very hot water and keep that shape. I rejected the plan because it aimed at selling a relatively undifferentiated product into an established consumer market, which is almost impossible. On the other hand I suggested that the product could be sold as a promotional item in a chain of fast food shops. Unfortunately the idea was rejected by the inventor ('too demeaning'). This is an imaginary conversation about what might have been.

I have called the marketing manager Gerry Grasshopper. In Aesop's fable of the grasshopper and the ant, the grasshopper is a typical Mover. The grasshopper flits around, is perennially optimistic, never worries about the future, and thinks with its heart and not with its head.

The individual concerned is an imaginary amalgam of several individuals I have met during my career. The incidents that occurred during this hypothetical conversation have all happened.

First Call on a Mover

The Mover

I was on my way to visit Mr Gerry Grasshopper, the marketing manager for Hamburger Hut, a leading chain of fast food outlets. Our company had developed a new toothbrush which you could bend under the hot water tap to any shape you wanted and when the plastic cooled down it would remain fixed in its new position. Children thought the toothbrushes were great fun and as kids are the decision-makers for fast food restaurants we thought we might be able to convince Hamburger Hut to use them for a marketing campaign.

I arrived at the head office of Hamburger Hut, which was hidden away off a freeway behind large trees. There were two receptionists at the desk and, between the constant phone calls, I managed to hand

11

across my card and announce my presence. People were everywhere. On the walls were motifs of various advertising campaigns and charities with which Hamburger Hut was involved. I joined the six other people waiting in reception.

Twenty minutes after the scheduled time for the appointment, a small man burst through the doors from the head office into the reception area. He was not wearing a coat. His sleeves were rolled up to his elbows and his collar was unbuttoned at the top.

'Hi, Donna. Where's the toothbrush man?'

'Over there in the grey suit and the blond hair.'

He strode across and breathlessly apologised for being late.

'Sorry, we just had an impromptu meeting of the social club. We are organising a horseriding weekend and somebody wanted the company to organise insurance. "Have a go," I said, "let people organise their own if they are worried." Now, it's Jim, isn't it?'

'Yes, Mr Grasshopper,' I said, extending my hand into a back.

Mr Grasshopper had spun around and was now talking to someone else.

'Bill, isn't it? Didn't we meet about three months ago at the Big Potato Golf Day?'

'Yes, Gerry, it was a great day wasn't it?'

'Terrific, met some great people. Say, why don't you pop down to my office when you are through and have a cup of coffee? I would love to talk with you — you wouldn't mind, would you Jim?' he said turning back to me and giving me another big smile.

'No trouble at all, Mr Grasshopper.'

'Call me Gerry, Jim. Everyone does.'

'Yes, Gerry,' I said, meanwhile thinking to myself that it really helps a sales presentation to have a complete stranger interrupt it in the middle for a cup of coffee.

We started to move across the reception area to the head office entrance when suddenly Gerry dashed back to the reception area.

'Any messages?'

'Yes, Gerry. We have two that have just come in. The advertising agency wants you to see the video of the new advert and a radio station wants to talk to you about a new programme that targets the children's market.'

'Right, well,' he looked at me then at his watch. 'Ring them and tell them I will ring them later.'

He turned round, gave me an emphatic come-on signal with his right hand and said, 'Well, it's 11.30. Let's get going.'

We burst through the door and sprinted down the hall to his office.

On the way Gerry said hello to seven people, three pot plants and one closing door.

We finally got to his office. Advertising boards were everywhere. A long, low filing cabinet had papers scattered across the top and his desk was filled with more files, knick-knacks, executive toys and telephone messages.

The phone rang. Gerry picked it up instantly.

'Gerry here. Hi Fred. How's the wife and kids? No. Yes. No. Look I'll ring you later. I have someone with me at the moment.'

Gerry then dialled his secretary on the hands-free phone. 'Roxie, will you take a drinks order please?'

'Get me a diet Coke. What will you have, Jim?'

'Oh, a natural spring water would be nice.'

'And hold the calls, Roxie,' said Gerry, pressing the disconnect button.

'I hate doing that but the boss says you have to focus on the job at hand.'

Gerry smiled at me and I smiled back.

'Right. Now what's this idea you've got? Will people like it?'

'Kids don't just like this toothbrush, Gerry, they love it!'

Profile of a Mover

It is easy to recognise people with reasonably strong Mover — they are always smiling. They are cheerful, outgoing, warm and enthusiastic. Because they are dominated by the desire to communicate they project optimism and relish social activity. They are the individuals who get up at 5:30 a.m. to go jogging with a group of friends. Movers will share in a car pool to commute to the office. After a workday full of meetings, the Mover then loves to take part in some active social entertainment in the evening such as a party or going to a discotheque.

Every so often there is a pause in this frenetic activity. An outburst of emotion will suddenly occur, accompanied by statements such as 'It's impossible — I can't go on. Nobody listens or cares after all I do for them.' This short piece of melodrama is soon over and forgotten, the batteries are recharged and the whirl of social activity restarts.

Movers are usually late for appointments because they are

always trying to do several things at once and are so easily distracted. They will quickly shake hands with you, putting their hands out first, give you a warm smile and immediately start calling you by your first name. They will socialise before coming to business, telling you of some personal incident of the previous night or earlier in the day. Their voices are quick and enthusiastic. They seem sanguine, buoyant and fidgety. The flow of Movers' conversation is changeable and will suddenly switch direction and they support their conversations with vigorous hand gestures. They answer the phone immediately if it starts to ring; they love distractions, especially if it means further social contact.

Movers start tasks enthusiastically yet often lack the concentration to finish, so their desks are usually cluttered. They tend to see issues in black and white and prefer action to thought. People sometimes criticise Movers for being impulsive and showing poor attention to detail, but if their decisions are successful, people forget the criticism and praise the Mover for rapid analysis and audacity.

Both male and female movers prefer casual clothes such as T-shirts, jeans and floppy sweaters. They like bright colours and can often be seen in bright plaids and patterns. The uniform of a Mover could be running shoes, jeans or bicycle riding shorts, a Ken Done pullover and a bright yellow button with a smile saying 'Don't Worry — Be Happy'.

Because they have sunny dispositions, yellow is the Mover colour. It is no coincidence that the largest fast food chain in the world, McDonalds, and the largest car rental company, Hertz, both have yellow as their colour.

In the office Movers quickly remove their coats and sometimes roll up their shirtsleeves. The men sometimes unbutton their collars and loosen their ties. The women prefer shorter hair as it is easier to maintain and wear simple natural make-up.

Anti-Movers appear to be cold, colourless and phlegmatic. Low Movers appear dull and drab and are at a distinct disadvantage in western society, in which the norms are based on social activity and contact.

On the other hand, people with a strong Mover component can sometimes be trying as individuals. They like and want to interact socially and need to receive affection in return. Some people consider they overreact and are too mercurial. Movers can be insensitive, too, in the way they force their optimism onto every-one else; their feverish imploring to 'cheer up and smile' can sometimes become tiresome.

Movers, because they need excitement and change, tend to switch jobs and friends easily — for them loyalty is a temporary feeling. As Movers may be mercurial both in personality and friendships, people sometimes suspect them of insincerity. This is unjust, however; the Mover will not deceive deliberately. Unfor-tunately Movers are so impulsive that they sometimes unwit-tingly hurt or offend more sensitive people.

Authors often choose Movers as characters; Jane Austen's Emma and the Mr Micawber of Charles Dickens are two good examples.

The 1920s was a Mover decade — the boom mentality, peren-nial optimism and the social whirl typify the Mover. The frenetic activity of the Charleston, the popularity of clubs and nightspots and the mergers in the business community in that era all indi-cate the dominance of the Mover component.

At work Movers may be disruptive, since they lack self-control. Their desire to communicate means that they may distract their fellow workers with conversation and chatter. They have a ten-dency to start a task with enthusiasm but their interest soon expires; they start evening courses, for example, and then leave after several weeks, and their backyards are full of half-finished boats. If you give them a deadline they usually fail to meet it. On the other hand, if you give them a job which requires meeting lots of people and having little responsibility or concern for tomorrow, they are excellent performers.

Successful business people often have a high Mover component and this provides them with the necessary energy, drive and enthusiasm. Successful people in sales, public relations or person-nel usually have a large amount of Mover component, too. The worst jobs for Movers are ones that coop them up in an office alone without a phone.

Selling to a Mover

If you were selling a car to a Mover, you would suggest a yellow station wagon (or perhaps a bus) saying how easy it would be to carry lots of people. You would give examples about how useful it would be on social occasions such as picnics, barbecues and football matches.

Your conversation to a Mover prospect or client should use phrases that appeal to his or her energy and desire to communicate and socialise; for example:

> 'You can feel the energy in this car . . .'
>
> 'Driving this will be a lot of fun for you and your family . . .'
>
> 'If you and your friends go to the beach, this car will be terrific . . .'
>
> 'Look how much space there will be to take your children and their schoolfriends to their Saturday sports meetings . . .'

In conclusion, Movers think with their hearts and not their heads. If you have a Mover as a prospect, then during the sale you must be as emotional as possible and throw logic out the window. Try to establish as much social contact as possible and show how the use of the product or service will increase the popularity of the buyer in the organisation.

*T*HE DITHERER

AFTER the desire to communicate, the next most common human desire is probably for security. The Ditherer is the stereotype in whom this desire is dominant. We all have some need for security in our personalities but for some this desire is stronger than others. In the following meeting I have used a prospect who is a pay-roll administrator. I met many people with a big Ditherer component when I was the national manager of the payroll services division of a major multinational company. Indeed I have even ended up marrying a person with 'big D'.

For both the preparation and maintenance of pay-roll information most organisations would prefer to employ somebody who has security uppermost in mind and who is also a compulsive double-checker of computer input and output. Most employees and organisations want to keep pay-roll and personnel information confidential; most managers also know that mistakes in a pay-roll can be a major cause of disharmony in an organisation.

I have chosen 'Rabbit' as the surname in this cameo because rabbits are timid creatures who, at the slightest hint of danger, tend to scurry off. Rachel Rabbit is a combination of three people I know.

First Call on a Ditherer

Rachel Rabbit was the senior pay officer for a large factory which had been built fifty years ago. Our company had recently done a mailing to promote our new pay-roll processing personal computer package. Ms

Rabbit had used a reply-paid card to request that we visit her.

I arrived five minutes early and was immediately directed to the pay office and shown in. The office had wall-to-wall filing cabinets and on each cabinet a metre-high pile of bound computer printouts was stacked. The desk was heaped with files. The room smelt of cigarette smoke and the ashtray was filled with butts. By the telephone was a photograph — of three children, a man and Ms Rabbit — which I guessed had been taken about three years ago.

The Ditherer

Ms Rabbit was wearing a brown cardigan over a tan dress. She had on little make-up and wore an expensive watch and a very expensive pair of glasses.

I handed across my card. Her handshake was weak.

'Oh, my youngest son is named Jim. My name is Rachel.'

'Good morning, Rachel. How's the day going?'

'Oh the usual disasters. The computer's down, the courier's late, I still have a terrible cough and the general manager wants a special labour costing report by tonight.'

'Not feeling well then?'

'No, there is a pain between my shoulders under my neck. These glasses are giving me a headache and my knee is playing up. Gosh, I just remembered.'

She poured out a glass of water. 'It's time for my pills.' From her desk drawer she took out three bottles.

'What are they all for?'

'The white ones are calcium, the brown ones are garlic and the green capsules are supercharged B vitamins.'

'Well, they should help you feel well. How's the family?'

'Oh I don't know. My youngest son just won't study and the eldest now wants to get married. I am worried about his girlfriend. She looks flighty to me. I'm sure it won't last.'

'Yes, well, it's a big decision and . . .'

Just then the phone rang. I waited. Rachel lit a cigarette.

'No . . . you can't be serious . . . this place is never going to survive another six months . . . I knew the old financial controller was given the push and the voluntary retirement was just a cover . . . Oh I don't know . . . we will just have to stick it out . . . How's your neck? My cough is still playing up. It must be the pollen in the air . . . Look I better hang up. I have someone with me. See you at lunch.'

'Good friend?'

'That was Madge in creditors. Just been told to pay no cheques for the next two weeks without the boss's signature. I tell you this company is going to be bankrupt by Christmas. Just my luck — the only fun I ever have is at the office party.'

'Well, I'm sure it can't be as bad as you think. Now you sent us a reply-paid card to come and see you. Are you having problems with your current supplier?'

'Problems? I knew I was rash when I chose them over five years ago. It has been a catastrophe. The staff are unprofessional. They are too slow to respond to customer requests and the software is riddled with bugs.'

'Riddled?'

'Yes, remember four years ago when they changed the tax scales?'

'Yes, I vaguely remember.'

'Well they had made a mistake in one of the cut-off points. It was $34,999 instead of $35,000, which meant employees would pay 1 cent more tax a week. Well, I was on the phone to them at least five times a day. It took them three days before it was fixed. All they could offer was the lame excuse that the government had made a typographical error in the schedules. They should have checked the original proclamation; it was there in black and white.'

'Any other problems?'

'Well, the staff are always changing. I get one pay-roll analyst then three months later she rings up and tells me she is being promoted or transferred and then I have get to know a new one.'

'You meet regularly?'

'Every week. I like to have a visit each week where we review the running of the previous week. We spend about an hour on it.'

'Oh.'

I thought to myself that my branch manager would love this since, once our system is installed, we budget for one meeting a month.

'Anything you dislike about the present reports?' I said, bracing myself.

'Well, where should we begin?' said Rachel, lighting another cigarette.

Profile of a Ditherer

The timid, nervous, indecisive civil servant best personifies the Ditherer. His or her primary drive is the desire for security. All through the day Ditherers imagine events that can go wrong and at night they dream of disasters.

Ditherers are easy to recognise. The haircuts of the men tend to be short back and sides and the women have conservative hair styles. Ditherers regard the safest place to be as on the ground and are often 'Earth Mother' types. Ditherers' favourite colours are brown and tan in clothes, fixtures and fittings in their houses and in office furniture. The men often wear brown ties or ties with crests representing membership of a large institution. The women carry large handbags full of make-up and accessories to cater for every possible occasion. They often carry a scarf or umbrella because it might get cold or rain. They usually have at least one picture of the family in the office and many in their homes. This is because Ditherers associate the family with security.

Ditherers are frequently dissatisfied with their lot in life and often complain or criticise. Many Ditherers are smokers, because smoking allows them to change their physical state temporarily. Someone, with gallows humour, has suggested that Ditherers become chain smokers to provide the opportunity to suffer from lung cancer. Meanwhile, smoking provides an explanation for the many imaginary ailments usually possessed by Ditherers, who are often hypochondriacs. Ask Ditherers how they feel today and in a few minutes you begin to wonder how they are alive!

The list of a Ditherer's illnesses often includes the following (at least):

- funny spasms in the neck;
- unusual fatigue;
- aching legs;
- indigestion and a funny stomach;
- migraine;
- internally bruised arms;
- twisted ankle;
- palpitating heart.

When reciting the above list, Ditherers frequently intersperse the items with deep sighs.

Female Ditherers are always snagging nails, having runny eyes or trouble with their hair. They have their teeth capped and are always changing glasses or contact lenses because the present ones are unsatisfactory. The outside observer sometimes suspects these troubles to be imaginary or trifling, because they are invisible. Ditherers fill the desks in their offices and the medicine chests in their homes with medicines to counter all types of imaginary ailments. Many of these nostrums should be thrown away, because they have long since lost any effectiveness, but Ditherers cannot bear to throw anything away in case it might be useful later.

In other words Ditherers are magpies and typically hoard everything in case it might come in handy. Hence their houses generally gather cupboards and chests while their offices accumulate filing cabinets.

Ditherers are customarily dissatisfied and like to complain. If something is not wrong with themselves then there is something wrong with work, friends or the house. The only time Ditherers cheer up is when they come across someone in a miserable state and really suffering. The Ditherer then shows an enthusiastic compassion which may appear morbid. The Ditherer will listen to every detail of the trouble, expressing sympathy at every opportunity, continually asking if the poor sufferer has told him everything. This capacity to listen to other people's misfortunes makes them good friends and in the office they often fulfil the role of a parent figure. The old saying 'Misery loves company' was coined with the Ditherer in mind!

When something eventually does go wrong the Ditherer tends to exaggerate it. Even if the matter is trifling, such as a seasonal decline in profits or late delivery of stock, the Ditherer will exaggerate the incident, typically as proof that the firm is on the verge of bankruptcy and will never be able to recover its tattered reputation. Even if the matter does not affect the present, the future effects will be calamitous. The Ditherer is always thinking about the future and how next year will be terrible. Ditherers so often project gloom that colleagues will sometimes refuse to work with them, citing reasons such as poor attitude and continual complaints.

Because Ditherers are so influenced by the desire for security and so dread possible calamities, they hesitate about making decisions for fear of the outcome. They tend to favour the status quo, especially if that means that little activity is needed. So Ditherers tend to appear mentally vague and physically inactive; they prefer to stay in bed because it is comfortable. Their innate anxiety and indecisiveness can make them seem passive and dull — when you have a conversation with a Ditherer the initial impression is often one of uncertain passivity.

Ditherers procrastinate over the smallest decision, going through both sides of the argument thoroughly. They will ask everyone for opinions, then equivocate and so disregard all the advice. This hesitancy, of course, frequently infuriates the givers of advice. They will also double-check every item of a proposal, use an outside expert to ensure accuracy and then ask for another draft in a different coloured binder.

As a general rule, Ditherers make excellent public servants. The employees of Ditherer managers become frustrated as nothing new ever seems to get done and every decision is so exhaustively reviewed that the cost of making the decision begins to outweigh the potential benefits. Government departments sometimes spend hundreds of thousands of dollars evaluating proposals which will cost less than the analysis, and even then end up with ambiguous solutions!

Ditherer employees tend to exasperate their superiors as they often ask for unnecessary approvals and sanctions.

The 1930s, the time of the Great Depression, was dominated

by the Ditherer mentality. The early part of the decade was characterised by governments failing to make decisions. Innovation in many areas stopped. The advertising and films of the era were filled with cigarettes and stressed security and quality. When Ditherers finally make a decision they tend to choose goods that are of the highest quality and good reputation. They justify this approach by reasoning that cheaper goods will deteriorate more quickly and that you can never go wrong if you choose good quality.

Ditherers often work in clerical and administrative positions. Their habit of double-checking everything makes them excellent employees in areas where accuracy is a requirement. Thus brown cardigans and filled ashtrays decorate the administration offices around the world.

Ditherers are notoriously slow starters and some people think their inert passivity is laziness. They will complain in the morning about doing the same task every day and usually need some encouragement to get going. Yet once they get into the swing of the task at hand, especially if it is familiar, they cheer up. The Ditherer is genuinely surprised to find that, at the end of the day, people still remember their bad humour and uncertainty of the early morning.

Too little Ditherer component in a personality leads to impulsive, reckless behaviour. Low Ditherers have little compassion for the suffering of others and have no misgivings about their actions. They tend to make decisions quickly and will often buy from the first salesperson they see.

As stated before, every individual has some degree of each of the seven temperament components in their personality. A later section will cover combinations, but the Mover-Ditherer combination is a common personality type. People with a strong Mover or Ditherer usually appear to have a reasonable degree of the other component because they share the same base personality factor — emotionalism. These people often describe themselves as being either up or down. As the name suggests, the two components tend to dominate behaviour alternately. At the extreme, a Mover-Ditherer can exhibit the moody, mercurial behaviour of the manic-depressive. The amount of time that either component controls the personality depends on its relative strength. However, at various times the other component will govern behaviour.

Selling to a Ditherer

If you were trying to sell a car to a Ditherer you would perhaps first take the prospect through the service area and show how the car keeps its resale value.

Ditherers prefer cars with a reputation for quality and reliability, such as Toyotas or Volvos. Indeed the brown Toyota is the stereotype Ditherer car, although a white Volvo (because white is a safer colour at night) would run it a close second.

Your conversation might concentrate on alleviating fear and satisfying the desire for security; for example:

'This car has a three-year, 60,000-kilometre warranty period . . .'

'This was chosen last year by the magazine *European Car* as the safest car yet produced.'

'The insurance premiums on this car are the lowest of its competitors because of its terrific safety record over the past three years.'

'Let's go and talk to our service manager. He will tell you that this is the most reliable car he and his team have ever worked on . . .'

'The braking system on this car is so advanced that it is almost impossible to skid.'

It is a difficult selling task to get Ditherers to make a decision, but a classic selling technique, because of the cyclic behaviour discussed above, is to approach them when they are on an upswing. This is not so difficult as it might appear. If you have a Ditherer prospect or are in a sales situation such as wholesaling that requires repetitive weekly calls, approach the Ditherer for a decision at the beginning of the week — preferably early on Monday morning. By the time the weekend is over the Ditherer will be dissatisfied with home and crave something different. On Monday the Ditherer will be in an upbeat mood, by Friday the optimism will generally have dissipated.

THE ARTIST

PSYCHOLOGICAL tests have postulated the presence of over twenty different personality factors. The first factor usually extracted in personality testing is the degree of emotion often shown by a person. Emotionalism underlies two connected temperament types, the Mover and the Ditherer. Both these types centre on feelings and emotions and how a person relates to his environment. Individuals who have a high degree of these two types in their personality react strongly to outside stimuli and are strongly influenced by their senses. They project energy outwards, in the form of optimism in the case of the Mover or of insecurity in the Ditherer.

The Mover and the Ditherer are both extrovert temperament components. It is time to discuss the introvert components — the Artist, the Politician, and the Engineer.

As we shall see later, most adults tend to have one influential extrovert component and one influential introvert component, along with average-to-strong Normal. If, on the other hand, the two dominant components are both introvert ones, then the person will tend to exhibit the introvert behaviour first characterised by Jung.

Introverts, as a rule, tend to be inward-looking people who care more for their own company than that of others. The Artist, Politician and Engineer all have the capacity to handle mental, abstract concepts, but besides having different dominant desires the three temperaments differ in the kinds of information they prefer to process and in how they think. In very general terms,

Artists are visual, Politicians are aural and Engineers are tactile.

It is the introvert component that influences the data and information processing of the individual.

Twenty thousand years before people began to farm or lived in cities, they had started to paint. In caves in Southern France and in Spain, for example, archaeologists have discovered cave paintings of superb quality. The creative desire is one of the most basic in mankind and if it is dominant it leads to the Artist stereotype. In the following discussion the Artist prospect is an architect and, again, a fusion of several people I have known. I have called him Mr Clam because Artists are generally so tight-lipped that they can be particularly awkward customers.

First Call on an Artist

I was on my way to see Clam and Coral, a leading architectural practice in the city. My appointment was with Mr Clarence Clam, a senior partner. Our company had developed an electronic security access control system for use in high-rise office blocks. Part of the company's marketing strategy was to 'sell' the product to the architects, who would in turn specify the system to the builders or developers. We had managed to persuade most of the city architects to specify our system, and after repeated phone calls, I had finally managed to get an appointment with Mr Clam.

The offices of Clam and Coral were located in a restored warehouse in an old quarter of the city. The office reception area was unusual as the walls had been stripped back to the original sandstone. The ceiling had also been removed and the old beams and rafters were visible. Hanging on the wall were drawings and photographs of buildings and some exceptionally colourful works of modern art. There was also what looked like a painted refrigerator.

The receptionist was wearing a dress with an unusual blend of colours and patterns and a pair of very exotic earrings. At exactly ten o'clock the receptionist was buzzed and she led me to the office of Mr Clam. Mr Clam's office was set in the corner of the building which caught the morning sun. As I walked in, the first item I noticed was a singular piece of modern sculpture in one corner. In another corner Mr Clam had put a large drawing easel. The office, because it was located in the corner of the building, had two large windows in adjoining walls. Mr Clam had positioned his desk in the corner which faced away from the spectacular views.

I approached his desk and, since he was still reading, coughed gently.

'Mr Clam, Jim Smith,' I said, handing across my card.

He looked at it for a few seconds, stood up and replied, as he slowly extended his hand, 'Yes, Mr Smith. How can I help you?'

His grip was loose and the handshake was short. We both sat down, he doing so rather quickly. As I slowly seated myself I noticed he was wearing a very modern French leather jacket over an expensive, open-necked, silk shirt. Underneath his thick beard he had tied a fashionable silk scarf around his neck.

'Good view.'

'Many people think so. Personally I find it rather distracting.' His voice was quiet, almost timid.

'Oh. Do you know anyone at Build and Better?'

'Yes. I have met M——,' he mumbled, with his hand over his mouth.

'Sorry. I didn't catch the name.'

'Mr Melrose.'

'Ah yes, Mike Melrose. Great guy. Good tennis player. Have you ever played tennis with him?'

The Artist

'No. I don't tend to socialise with other architects. Too many are show-offs or have tunnel vision.'

'Oh, but you know his work?'

'Yes.'

'The Winchester Town Hall was one of his. What did you think of that?'

'Good.'

'Good?'

There was a long pause. I had so far not made eye contact with Mr Clam. I then noticed that I was leaning forward in my chair. I sat back rather noisily, crossed my legs, put my elbows on the arms of the chair, and joined my hands in an extended prayer position in front of my face.

Mr Clam looked me in the face for the first time and said, in a slightly relaxed voice, 'I thought the use of perspective in the atrium very imaginative.'

'Anything else?'

'Beyond a shadow of a doubt it is an outstanding building.'

I slowly realised that the ten phone calls it had taken to make this appointment had been the easy part.

Profile of an Artist

The Artist is dominated by the desire to create. Genesis was a solitary affair and since that time creation has usually been a lonely activity. Artists often appear as quiet, shy, withdrawn people. They are easy to recognise because they avoid eye contact, the males often have beards and they are initially tongue-tied. As they talk, Artists tend to put their hands over their mouths or faces. They appear to wish to avoid socialising or contact with the environment. If an Artist has an office with a spectacular view the desk is sometimes positioned so the view cannot be seen — Artists prefer the creative imagination to reality.

Artists tend to use visual words such as 'clear', 'show', 'appears' and 'look'. They also use visual expressions such as:

'I get the *picture*.'
'I *see* what you mean.'
'That's a *sight* for sore *eyes*.'
'I take dim *view* of that.'
'In the *light* of . . .'
'Let's put things into *perspective*.'

As Artists have good visual imaginations their dress sense is creative and colourful. Thus Artist men wear unusual ties and both sexes will tend to be the first to adopt new, imaginative fashions. Their offices, while neat and tidy, are usually visually creative and full of strong, vivid colours. Artists make good interior designers, architects and, of course, painters. Vincent van Gogh was a classic case and displayed how individualistic Artists can be when he mutilated his ear!

The first conversation with an Artist is often strained. They do not mix easily and tend not to use first names till they have met you several times. They will not talk about themselves or their families and, if they have self-control, they seem cold and aloof. People sometimes think Artists are snooty but the opposite is true. Artists are easily embarrassed and often have feelings of such social inferiority that they prefer to avoid social contact. They are asocial rather than anti-social and usually have few friends.

Artists are difficult prospects. They have been likened to clams, but clams seem to lead dull and boring lives while Artists, because of their lively and colourful imaginations, have a pleasant time day-dreaming and meditating in flights of fancy. If this behaviour becomes too dominant the individual may withdraw completely from society.

Meditation, beards, imaginative clothes, inarticulate mumbling and socially indifferent behaviour were the characteristics of the Woodstock generation of the 1960s, so the most successful sales techniques with Artists are those that emulate the advertising of that period. Appeals to being part of a group and how to improve your status are out — appeals to the imaginative, internal self are in. The most successful advertising slogan of all time — 'We're number two but we try harder' — was created in the 1960s and is a classic appeal to an Artist. Few firms would publicly admit that they are number two or suggest to the prospect that part of the buying process is to imagine which car rental firm would try harder.

Artists, because of their sensitivity and imagination, are able to empathise well with other individuals. They tend to be thoughtful and sensitive and will avoid hurting people. Artists will avoid social embarrassment, however, so they work best in solitary positions. With high intelligence they often make good general managers, if few decisions have to be made and conflicts are rare. Avoidance of conflict is another goal of the Artist.

People sometimes mistake the quiet of the Artist for timidity. Because the Artist hates to argue, especially in a group, opponents or salespeople often believe that they have won an argument only to discover the opposite later. Artists can be stubborn and, once they have made up their minds, they are almost impossible to change. They can become dogged in their attitudes and almost rocklike in their silent refusal to accept a change of view. If their feelings are hurt Artists can carry the desire for revenge for a long time and, even if the offence was unintentional or imaginary, still be recalcitrant.

Because of their visual orientation and creative desires Artists like to go to films, art galleries and museums. They sometimes have posters of these on the wall or programmes on their desks or coffee tables. Another clue is fresh flowers, which are often in a distinctive vase.

People usually consider Anti-Artists as hard, cold and insensitive. They are usually blunt, direct people who appear to lack finesse. Because they are unaware of social niceties and indifferent to social disapproval, they make good salespeople to large organisations in competitive businesses. Low Artists will usually lack creativity and the ability to visualise new ideas.

Artists are sensitive to all the colours. Of the colours of the spectrum violet, or more particularly the delicate mauve, is one of the most unusual. It is a colour that Artists often use to telling effect.

Artists prefer cars that are both stylish and individualistic, such as Saabs or Citroens. Indeed a purple Saab coupe (four door sedans are too inviting to crowds) would be perfect.

Selling to an Artist

If you were trying to sell a car to an Artist you would tend to point out the technical and design features of the automobile and suggest that the Artist imagines the benefits. You should also use visual language when making benefit statements; for example:

'Dream about how easy this car will be to drive along country roads.'

'Can you imagine why the designers did not put the ignition switch on the steering column?'

'Picture the expressions on your family's faces when you drive up in this new car.'

Make liberal use of visual aids, too, such as brochures, videotapes or photographs. The trick is to let the prospect look at the various items and not to interrupt while he or she is processing and considering the images.

If a salesperson making a quick one-off sale is confronted with an Artist as a prospect, the best option may be to go and find another prospect. If, however, the sale is one which should lead to a long relationship with many repeat orders then the salesperson should persist. Artists like time to consider and may suggest adaptations of a proposal which are impractical. Occasionally, however, the suggestion is successful and unusually creative. Artists are often detached from reality, yet they are the people who cause progress, because of their refusal to accept conventions. They often have a narrow range of interests which they attach creatively to all new concepts. They will listen to proposals and suggestions with a calm, passive demeanour and after a presentation the salesperson will be unsure if the sales call has been successful. The best approach with an Artist is to realise that the first sale will be slow and will require patience. The reward is that, once the salesperson has established a relationship, the competition will find it impossible to break.

CHAPTER 6

THE POLITICIAN

THE desire to win is so widespread among human beings that it is often called the 'competitive instinct'. Whether the desire to win is instinctive or learned is a matter for debate but the amount of human resources which are devoted to competitive sport all over the world, from children's school sport to the Olympics, testifies to the desire to win. We all have some degree of this desire in us. I have named the stereotype of a person dominated by a desire to win the 'Politician'. It is unfortunate that the terms 'political' and 'politician' now have undertones of stealth and evasive behaviour, probably because of Machiavelli and most people's experience, either personally or through the media, that political power may corrupt.

However politics can be seen as a game. It is about winning power. Countries where the game is played regularly, according to agreed rules, and where the people are the judges, are called 'democracies'. The Politician stereotype is a person dominated by the desire to win, not a sinister Machiavellian.

In the cameo below I used the surname 'Tiger'. Again this person is a combination of several people I have met, all of whom were running large organisations.

First Call on a Politician

I had now been waiting in the foyer of the head office building of the State Electricity Commission for over thirty minutes. Not that it was an uncomfortable wait. The State Electricity Commission building, like that of many public utilities, was one of the largest and most imposing buildings in the city. The foyer, complete with wall fountains and tapestries, tall indoor palms, and Italian leather lounges, was the most opulent in the city.

I was a partner in a consulting company that specialised in training and organisational development. I had an appointment to see Ms Teresa Tiger, the head of personnel, at 10 a.m. It was now 10.25 and still no one had appeared.

The Politician

Suddenly I was beckoned across by a receptionist. Waiting for me was a young, neatly dressed girl who was introduced as Ms Tiger's secretary. The secretary said that Ms Tiger would see me now and asked me to accompany her to the lift. We went up to the top floor, through the equally imposing head office foyer, through a security door, then down a set of large circular marble steps which had been built to join the two top floors. We walked to a corner office and I was asked to sit down and wait.

Five minutes later a woman in her mid-thirties appeared.

'Ms Tiger?'

'No, no. I am Ms Tiger's personal assistant. Follow me please.'

She took me through the secretary's office and into her office which was about twice the size. She went up to a door, knocked twice and waited. About thirty seconds later there was an authoritative 'Enter' and she went inside. She came out about five minutes later.

'Ms Tiger will interview you now.'

I strode purposefully into the office and nearly tripped as my feet sank into several centimetres of thick pile. Ms Tiger was seated at the far end of the room at one of the largest desks I had ever seen. The personal assistant led me across the office. While we trekked across, I could not help noticing a number of degrees, awards and plaques on the walls. Underneath one plaque was a photo of her with the previous Premier of the State.

As we walked up to the desk Ms Tiger remained sitting. The personal assistant handed across my card.

'Mr Smith, may I introduce Ms Tiger?'

'Everyone calls me Jim,' I said as I held out my hand.

'Everyone, except for a few close, important friends, calls me Ms Tiger,' she said as she stood up and shook my hand with a firm, dry handshake.

'Sit down, Mr Smith,' she said as she handed across her card.

'Susan, would you please hold all calls. I am not to be disturbed unless it is particularly urgent.'

While this command was being given I looked at her card. Ms Tiger was the proud holder of three degrees and a member of two organisations. She was dressed in a simple, classical charcoal grey suit and a grey blouse. She was in her mid-forties and was wearing simple earrings and expensive German steel-framed glasses.

'I've heard you belong to the Association of Training Officers.'

'I was the President three years ago.'

'Oh, I didn't realise. We moved here from the East Coast two years ago.'

'In addition, I was the recipient in the following year of the inaugural prize for the individual who had done the most to promote industrial training in the state during the previous twelve months. On the wall is a photograph of me accepting the prize from the former State Premier, who is a charming man.'

I turned around and looked at the photograph.

'The idea for the prize was devised by me while I was president of the Association and awarded to me the following year. It also carries with it life membership of the Association.'

'Congratulations.'

'Thank you. Well, Mr Smith, what is your position in the company you represent? Are you the managing partner?'

'No — we don't have one. We operate as a true partnership. We have a managing committee and the chairperson rotates monthly. I was made a partner when I left my professorship five years ago.'

'Oh. Why did you leave university?'

'For several reasons. But to tell the truth, I suppose I wanted to prove that some of those who teach can also do.'

'Did you publish anything?'

'Heaps — and I did collaborate on several papers. Probably the most famous is Jackson and Smith's "Preferred Structures for Computer Based Training Modules".'

'That rings a bell. Of course I have heard of it — so you are that Smith. That was an excellent paper. Look, you must come and address the next meeting of the State Personnel Managers Society. I'm the current president. We will have to postpone the planned talk but don't you worry about that.'

Just then the telephone rang.

Ms Tiger pressed the hands-free button.

'Yes, Susan?'

'It's Mr Counter, Head of Financial Administration. He says it's urgent.'

'This better be serious, Mr Counter. I am in the middle of an important meeting.' A few minutes of company discussion then followed between Ms Tiger and Mr Counter. She hung up and returned to me.

'I shouldn't tell you this and be a tattletale but last week he missed a very important heads of department meeting I called about introducing a new personnel policy. He will live to regret that snub, I promise you.'

I nodded understandingly.

'Well, Mr Smith, in your opinion exactly what help do you consider your company can provide for my organisation?'

Profile of a Politician

In the same way that the Mover is the antithesis of the Ditherer, so the Politician is the opposite of the Artist. Verbal rather than visual, Politicians tend to have fixed opinions which they force on others aggressively. Unfortunately they can be so competitive in social discourse that they sometimes appear boastful and conceited.

35

As these are not popular traits, Politicians who lack a strong Normal component can offend their colleagues. If they have a limited desire for social approval and lack self-control, Politicians will respond with more aggression and truculence in the face of social censure. However, if the Politician has good self-control, the desire to win often results in leadership.

The Artist tends to avoid social gatherings and, if forced to attend, may retreat into a shell. By contrast Politicians, who love any form of games or sport, prefer those social contacts which they consider will provide an opportunity to engage in competitive conversations and discussions.

The language of the Politician centres around auditory words. Below are some examples:

'I *hear* you *loud* and *clear* but I will have to *discuss* this decision with my peers.'

'That name *rings a bell* with me. To *tell* you the truth I never paid much attention to that company.'

'That product *sounds* interesting. Would you please describe it in more detail.'

'I will *tell* you who makes the decisions in that area. Now *listen* carefully to what I am going to say.'

'The problem with most salespeople is their inability to *communicate*.'

'I am *telling* you to match your competitor's service contract *word for word*.'

The dominant use of sound words in conversation is a good indicator of the Politician component.

You can quickly recognise the self-importance of Politicians; they generally keep you waiting for an appointment. A Politician's desk is often placed diagonally across the corner opposite the entrance to the office or in some other dominant position. Degrees, awards, and pictures of teams with the Politician in the centre as captain frequently hang on the office walls. Politicians tend to be formal and not use first names unless they also have a strong Mover or Hustler component.

Once they give an opinion or an instruction Politicians so want to win and so hate to lose that they often stick stubbornly to their initial statement. One example of the mulish behaviour of a Politician I can remember was during a sales meeting. The Politician prospect had instructed his secretary to take all telephone calls. Halfway through the presentation the telephone on his desk began to ring. He continued to talk, letting the telephone ring and ring. After at least five minutes, when all around him were desperate to pick up the telephone, the ringing finally stopped. The Politician acted as if nothing unusual had happened and continued talking about what he had achieved for his employer over the past five years.

Politicians naturally have a high opinion of themselves. Their conversation is egocentric. 'I'll tell you what I think' and 'I said' are frequent phrases. Often their opinions are not only fixed but also biased.

Politicians enjoy arguments and discussions which they often win because they are good at expressing themselves. They interpret facts to suit themselves and their tenacious beliefs. The Pope who conferred infallibility on himself was a true Politician. As a perceptive aphorist once said: 'You can always tell a Politician, but you cannot tell him much'.

Another trait Politicians have is to adopt another person's ideas and use them as their own. This trait is very useful for a sales executive who can sow the seeds of product features and let them germinate into benefits.

The self-righteousness of the Politician can be very irritating to other people. Politicians often give unsolicited advice and make comments about issues that do not concern them. Because of their strong desire to win, they strive to gain positions that will improve their status and prestige.

Unfortunately organisations sometimes promote Politicians above their competence (the Peter Principle) and they then become bossy and domineering towards everyone reporting to them. They resent any questioning of their authority and antagonistic arguments may follow. A Politician in this position habitually talks about lines of authority and then either breaks or disregards them.

Not only do Politicians like to win, they also like to show other people that they have won. They hanker after signs of authority. Just as the South American dictators have medals emblazoned on their chests, the business card of a Politician usually contains a string of letters. Politicians need respect and admiration and believe such trappings help them. Unfortunately, they can become suspicious of their colleagues and a mild form of paranoia may set in. Office memos may start to flow, because Politicians are good at office warfare. Politicians may become increasingly impervious to reason, maintaining that counter-arguments are false. They can end up by believing that everyone else is wrong and too dumb to understand the 'truth'.

Because they hate to lose, Politicians are good at shifting blame to other people if mistakes occur. They will hold a grudge for a long time, too. If forced to do something against their wishes by someone with more authority, Politicians will often do the task unwillingly and under protest.

Not only do Politicians want signs of authority, they want positions of authority. They will join clubs and soon try to run the whole show. Unlike Movers, who crave the social contact, Politicians regard organisations as another game and the person who gets to the top as the winner.

Because they are capable of supporting bizarre causes, Politicians can transform society. Their absolute confidence in their own beliefs and intolerance of opposing views means that they are often in the vanguard of change in society. On the other hand, their need for status and power often means that they join intrinsically conservative organisations such as the armed forces or the police so that they can exercise authority. Politicians often become the chief executives of large organisations and unions.

One classic Politician stereotype is the left-wing shop steward who is suspicious of any proposition made by management. As stated in the introduction, Politicians are also common in government — think of a prime minister or a president and you are usually thinking of a Politician.

A leader's personality should contain a lot of the Politician component. Without it, the instability in decision making would be too disruptive. The stable opinions of the Politician, which he or she can usually state forcefully and with self-assurance, are most important to organisational development. This is because organisations will succeed if they have goals and stick to them; it often does not matter whether the goals are correct. Even if defeated several times, Politicians will persistently keep returning to the battle and this is what makes them so competitive in sport, politics and business.

If, however, the Politician lacks self-control and maturity, he or she may be a problem as a leader. Those reporting to the Politician may argue and then leave. The departures will be bitter and cause resentment and concern to those still reporting to the Politician. Politicians can sometimes tend to be too domineering in employee relationships and people often accuse them of being little dictators.

Politicians tend to take personal credit for the successes of their department but ensure that failures are shared co-operatively or blamed on an underling.

The person with little Politician component is a good follower, unprejudiced and compliant. There is no fear of an Anti-Politician leading a coup d'etat. Indeed, if Anti-Politicians are put in positions of authority, they may prove failures as they will vacillate over decisions and fail to inspire those beneath them. Faced with even mild opposition, they will crumble. They lack the competitive spirit which selling requires. It is easy to deflect Anti-Politicians from current tasks and they often fail to follow through on work started.

Blue is the Politician's colour — a colour adopted by many conservative political parties. Many observers would regard IBM as one of the most successful competitive organisations in the world and blue is prominent in the colours of its machines and marketing material. IBM marketing executives have gained notoriety for their preference for blue pin-striped suits. It is not for nothing that IBM is called by its competitors and the computer media 'Big Blue'.

The 1940s was the decade of the Politician. Dress commonly consisted of a uniform and the constant conflict and aggression of that decade is the behaviour typical of Politicians. Even when World War II was over it was followed by spy trials and purges on both sides. The most popular form of dancing was the jitterbug, which some contemporaries saw as being less of a dance and more of throwing your partner around the room.

Selling to a Politician

Selling to a Politician is relatively easy, as we shall discover in the second half of the book. Perhaps the hardest task in selling is getting a decision and the Politician makes decisions easily. The decisions may be subjective and biased but at least they are made quickly.

As Politicians like to use sound words, the Empathy Salesperson will use sound words and techniques to reinforce the benefits of the product.

If you were a car salesperson selling to a Politician you could use some of the following techniques. First ask the Politician what car he or she drives and what people said about it when it was first bought. The most likely answer would be a blue Mercedes or a top-of-the-range, fully optioned Ford. The next step would be to ask the Politician whether he or she agreed with those other people's opinions. This would provide you with some idea of the features and benefits which you should concentrate on in your presentation. Then choose a car or model which the Politician thinks would raise his status in the eyes of his peers.

Next either use references:

'Read what this edition of *Motor Car* says about this car. It states it is the best buy on the market.'

or sound metaphors and phrases:

'Listen to this engine, it purrs like a kitten.'

'The sound-proofing and design of this car is so good you can hear the clock tick.'

'The doors fit perfectly. They don't make a sound when you close them.'

Then structure the sales presentation as a series of subordinate closes such as:

'Do you like white or blue as a colour?'
'Do you prefer automatic or manual?'
'Do you want power or normal steering?'

The Politician is fond of expressing opinions and the sale should follow quickly.

*T*HE ENGINEER

THE third of the introvert temperament components is the Engineer. Engineers are people who are dominated by the desire to complete inspired projects. I have called this stereotype the Engineer because that is how many engineers view their work — as builders of something useful that requires creative inspiration.

Engineers often become so possessed by what they are doing that they shut out the rest of the world. People who lack this characteristic of fierce concentration tend to regard Engineers as absent-minded and too theoretical, when they are in fact the most practical of all temperament types in their ability to complete tasks. Engineers do not only work in the construction industry; they are also common in businesses where the work is project-orientated such as software, commercial law and product design. I have met many people with big Engineer components both when I was a software systems engineer with IBM and now as a director of three hi-tech companies with relatively large research and development departments.

Again, the prospect in this cameo, Mr Beaver, is an amalgamation of several people. The beaver is an animal who spends all its life building dams and lake dwellings. A beaver will always complete a dam once it starts to build one, and once built the dam never breaks.

First Call on an Engineer

McIntosh and Jones was a leading industrial project design company specialising in chemical process plants. The head office was located in a low modern building in a new industrial estate set back among the trees. I was to see Mr Barry Beaver, the chief engineering manager, to discuss the possible purchase of a new flatbed plotter our company had developed.

I arrived five minutes early. The reception area contained several models of refineries and chemical plants. There were also at least twenty photographs of various manufacturing plants neatly and evenly spaced on the walls.

The receptionist buzzed Mr Beaver and I was given a plastic visitor's badge and told to proceed to the top level where Mr Beaver was waiting for me. He was of medium build with short hair and glasses. His shirtsleeves were rolled up to the elbow. There was a row of coloured pens and pencils in the left-hand pocket of his shirt. His tie was a simple blue and grey striped pattern.

The Engineer

We shook hands.

'Mr Beaver?'

'Yes. Call me Barry. Look, I'm sorry, the receptionist told me your name but I was involved with something else when she rang. Your name has slipped my mind.'

'Smith. Jim Smith,' I said as I handed across a card.

He looked at it for a moment then turned suddenly and started walking.

'Come on, let's get going. Time is money, you know.'

We arrived at his office, which was at the end of the corridor, and he ushered me in. I don't think I have ever seen an office more crammed with books and paper. One wall contained a bookshelf which reached from floor to ceiling and was packed with books. On the opposite wall he had pinned a large planning chart, which was full of arrows and activities, alongside a whiteboard. The whiteboard was also filled with figures, drawings and equations.

We sat down at his desk, which was packed with piles of files and working papers. He opened a drawer, rummaged around and, with a triumphant smile, produced a business card.

'I knew a packet of cards was in there. Everyone chips me about my desk but I know where everything is. I find it unbearable when my secretary tries to tidy it up.'

By now I was beginning to notice the flat, dry tone of Barry's voice. It reminded me of the voice synthesisers you hear in modern lifts or from personal computers. Just then the phone rang.

'Excuse me, Jim,' he said as he picked up the phone. 'Yes . . . what do you mean the manuals haven't arrived? That's impossible, damn it!'

For the first time Barry's voice rose — he was definitely annoyed.

'This is the third time in a fortnight we have been promised these manuals and an update software tape. This is the final straw. We are never going to buy anything from that computer company again. I want you to get in touch with their Chief Executive Officer every half hour until we have those manuals. The delay's killing us — we've got ten drafting staff and three design engineers hanging around doing nothing and we've slipped three weeks behind on the critical path. We can't afford the cost or the time slippage.'

He slammed down the phone and several pieces of plastic shot into the air.

'Damn, I think I broke the telephone.'

'Well, that's easily fixed.'

'Yes, but it's a hassle.'

'What's the problem?'

'Oh it's to do with a new project we are working on. I had decided it was time to upgrade our engineering design systems with new work stations. They were meant to be compatible with the old ones. Well they're not and our data base of drawings is inaccessible. Everyone was really enthusiastic about the new stations. The exterior design is good. Now we are beginning to wonder if we made a mistake.'

43

There was a knock at the door.

'Yes?'

'Your phone doesn't appear to be working, Mr Beaver.'

'Oh yes. Come in, Jane.'

She walked in carrying a glass of water and a packet of Alka-Seltzer.

'How many?'

'Two, I think, Jane, thank you.'

She dropped two tablets in the water and walked out. As the tablets started to effervesce Barry began to talk.

'We had our annual local Engineering Society dinner last night and we all got a little high. I don't generally drink to excess but you have to let your hair down occasionally. I must admit I can't remember the taxi ride home nor getting into bed.'

'Well, a good night recharges the batteries.'

'Absolutely — now, what is this hot device you are going to show me? Have you got a brochure or manual yet?'

Profile of an Engineer

As stated in the introduction, the Engineer's main desire in life is to complete inspired projects. If the Engineer cannot do something inspired, then completing a project is the next best reward. The office of an Engineer is easy to recognise by the filled bookcase and the project control chart on the wall. The desk is not always neat but the Engineer knows where everything is. They can become upset if they find their office or working area changed or altered. Although they are plodding, deliberate and thorough, Engineers are very enthusiastic when inspired.

Another characteristic of Engineers is their prodigious drinking, about which they frequently reminisce, especially when they were at university.

Engineers are active people who like to be outdoors. They like to play sport and are the ones who are often seen jogging around the roads and parks in the mornings, lunchtimes or evenings. When in the office they tend to stand up and stretch often. Nevertheless as they get older their tendency to drink combined with less exercise often leads to obesity. They also often have hobbies which involve building or testing things and they are often the first people to try a new product.

Engineers prefer to do one thing at a time in an orderly fashion. They spend their time creating projects and then completing them. If the project is sufficiently inspiring the Engineer can go into ecstasy and the resulting task can be so burned into the personality that it becomes a dominating influence. The Engineer will then attack the task with a doggedness which may ensure success but can also result in a blind obsession.

If Engineers become frustrated in doing a task, they can become tense and upset. They become complaining, fussy people who may suddenly explode — indeed their frustration can sometimes transform itself into violent physical rages. This irritability causes Engineers to be loners — they tend to try to complete projects themselves and find it difficult to delegate responsibility. The former USA President, Jimmy Carter, was a classic Engineer. He had been a former officer/engineer on a nuclear submarine and it is said that while he was President he even used to organise the bookings of the White House tennis court.

As stated before, Engineers are deliberate and single-minded and dislike interruption. They love to read about a subject thoroughly. They devote great attention to detail and their crammed bookshelves are usually a good clue to their personality.

Another clue is their monotonous tone of voice in conversation — Engineers tend to be pedants and to go on and on about the same topic. They may drive their listeners into a coma-like submission. Their conversation is self-centred and they love to talk about their achievements. These achievements may be impressive if the Engineer component is allied to some talent or intelligence. Some great figures in history, such as Alexander the Great, Julius Caesar and Mohammed, are examples of Engineer-dominated personalities. If the Engineer is an individual of scant intelligence or talent, then the personality can appear over-fussy and difficult. Another clue is that Engineers have strong likes and dislikes. However, unlike Politicians and Artists, you can sway an Engineer's opinions by the force of either inspired or detailed argument.

Engineers like to test or trial a product or service before they buy. They prefer to get involved physically with the product. This desire to get information by feeling the product and desire for activity is reflected in their language, which is peppered with action and feeling words.

'I don't *feel warm* about the product.'

45

'*Lay* your cards on the table and give me some *concrete* examples. I can't get to *grips* with the benefits.'

'Before this company *embraces* your service it will have to get some sense of the risks involved and make sure there is a *plan* in place for a smooth *implementation*.'

'To *push* this proposal through I will have to *pull* some strings. The top management here are hard-headed and need to be comfortable that the *change-over* will not be too much hassle.'

People weak in the Engineer component tend to be careless and bored with repetitious work. People generally criticise Anti-Engineers for not being persistent and objective enough. People with low Engineer component have limited powers of analysis and tend to diffuse themselves over many tasks. Anti-Engineers dislike planning. Anti-Engineers prefer to behave in a reactive fashion.

The 1950s was the Engineers' decade. These were the years of great scientific projects such as the H-Bomb, satellites in space and vaccines based on thorough testing. Some people called the 1950s the 'sleeping decade' because of the placid, nonrevolutionary behaviour of the students. The conformity and monotony of the 1950s even extended to the music — it was then that rock and roll, with its monotonous beat and lyrics, began.

Green, particularly in England, is the colour of the Engineer. British racing green is the colour in which British sports cars race. Also much of the 'green' environment movement is led by people in whom the Engineer component is either dominant or influential. Engineers enjoy activities which combine the outdoors, completion of a task, and solitude, such as bushwalking, rock climbing or canoeing. A major reason for the success of the 'green' movement is the dedication and persistence of its leaders and these are two of the characteristics of the Engineer.

Selling to an Engineer

The Engineer is an uncommon personality type. When you have one as a sales prospect you should aim at providing him or her with a solution that contains two things: as much detail as possible and a list of product features.

If you were selling a car to an Engineer you would spend a lot of time talking about engine displacements, torques, drag co-efficients and so on. You would aim at selling a car with a reputation for advanced engineering such as a BMW or Porsche. You would suggest a test drive and get the Engineer to run his hands over the green body paint. You would open up the bonnet and discuss each component in some detail. By discussing response times, tensions, flows and other active processes within the car you will find some unusual detail that will fascinate and attract the Engineer. Once you find the hot button it becomes a simple task to go on and develop empathy with the Engineer.

CHAPTER 8

*T*HE HUSTLER

W E now come to the last of the extrovert components — the Hustler. The Hustler stereotype is an individual driven solely by a desire for material success. Few people are completely devoid of a desire for wealth — most of us have at some time wanted a new car or a new item of clothing. Much of modern advertising is directed towards stimulating this desire, so it is not surprising that it is so prevalent.

Middlemen and brokers need to have a lot of Hustler in order to succeed. I have worked for nine years in the financial services industry and have met many brokers. Stockbrokers live by commission and have to create a market. To the questions 'Should I sell?' and 'Should I buy?' the broker must answer yes in both instances. Brokers are sometimes accused of being two-faced; to pay the alimony they have to be.

In the short sketch that follows I have chosen as a prospect a real estate agent who is a composite of several people I know. I have called him Mr Fox, since, traditionally, the fox is a shrewd, crafty character. I am sure that you, like me, will be familiar with several people who have some Hustler influence in their personality.

First Call on a Hustler

I was on my way to see Fox and Crow, real estate agents located in the main street. My appointment was with Frederick Fox, whom I understood to be the general manager. We were to discuss the

48

possible purchase by Fox and Crow of a personal computer based sales information and accounting system our firm had developed for real estate agents.

I managed to find a parking space down the street from their office and as I walked towards it I could not help noticing how their bright yellow and red sign stood out from the rest.

I walked in. The receptionist was a tinted blonde wearing a tight, red, sleeveless dress over a good figure. She had a deep tan and was wearing gold bracelets on both arms and rings on three fingers of each hand. She gave me a warm, friendly smile and when I introduced myself, said, 'Ah yes, sit down. Mr Fox is expecting you.'

The Hustler

I sat down on the red, yellow and brown lounge with my eyes slightly squinting from the burnished orange carpet. Right on time, Mr Fox strolled into the reception area.

'Jim, isn't it?' he said as he extended his hand and gave me another warm, friendly, toothpaste smile.

'Yes, Mr Fox,' I said shaking his hand. His handshake was firm and slightly prolonged.

'No, no, everyone calls me Fred. He looked down at my card. Isn't

Ted Tiger your MD? I played golf with him several weeks ago. Great guy.'

I nodded.

'Come this way into my office. It's at the back where I like it. This way I have to walk backwards and forwards past the staff and I can see who's working and who's playing around.'

We went into the main office and as he closed the door he put his arm around my shoulder and murmured, 'Mind you, I wouldn't mind playing around with that receptionist, would you?'

I nodded in agreement perhaps a little too vigorously and hastily.

On the way through the main office Fred caught me looking at the sales commission board.

'Those are our quarterly budgets. Besides the standard commissions we have our own special competition. The one at the top gets to take the spouse out to the best restaurant in town — the one at the bottom becomes externally redeployed.'

'We have something similar at our office.'

'Oh yes, and what position are you?'

'Oh, at the top,' I replied, somewhat stretching the truth as our competition had only started that week and nobody had runs on the board.

'Good. I only buy from winners.'

Just before we entered Mr Fox's office a salesman yelled out, 'Fred. Fine Cotton came in at six to one!'

'Terrific — that's $300. You play the sport of kings, Jim?'

'Occasionally, Fred. Fine Cotton? Where have I heard that name?'

'Oh it's a famous horse that was substituted in a big race in Brisbane a while ago. Fine Cotton is a country hack. Well I got the inside dope so I backed it on the tote so I wouldn't have any bookies chasing me for a refund if the switch was found out. It's beautiful — I have now made money on both the real Fine Cotton and the false one.'

We both laughed as we sat down. Fred's desk was neat and tidy. There were two pictures on the desk. One was of two kids and no wife. The other was of Fred shaking hands with an older gentleman and receiving a plaque. Under the second photograph was the notation 'Best Salesman in the Country 199–'. On one wall was a poster saying 'Money is not everything, but it sure comes a close second to whatever is.'

There was a moment's silence as we sized each other up. Fred was wearing a grey suit which had a slightly glittering thread running through it and a bright red striped tie with a designer label. On his left wrist was what looked like a Cartier watch and on his right a chunky gold bracelet. He was also wearing tinted glasses.

Behind him on the wall was a big oil painting that looked like a Johnson, one of the better known modern artists being talked about in the Sunday arts pages. I looked at the painting but could not see the distinctive Johnson signature which was always placed in the top left corner. Fred saw me looking at the painting.

'What do you think?'

'Well,' I said, 'It looks like a Johnson but I can't . . .'

'Can't see the signature — well it's an original copy. I had a local artist do it for me.'

'Ah, that explains it — uh, it's very good.'

'Yeah — Johnson was my ex-wife's favourite painter. Still this talk isn't making either of us any money. Now what does this system on which you are going to give me a 10 per cent discount exactly do?'

Profile of a Hustler

The Hustler is easy to recognise — just look at the advertising of the 1970s when Hustlers were the role models. The most common clue to the presence of a Hustler is the glitter and flashiness of the dress. Hustlers tend to wear overstated jewellery and exaggerated clothes. Hustler women often wear large earrings and costume rings on at least three fingers. The dresses will glitter with streaks of red, orange or gold. Hustler men will wear bracelets, gold chains hung around the neck, unbuttoned shirts or red or orange ties. Because Hustlers like signs of material success their clothes often carry designer labels or insignia.

Another clue that helps you to recognise the Hustler is the friendly, genial smile. Of all the stereotypes Hustlers are the most charming and certainly the most entertaining company. Another characteristic is their constant eye contact — they never look away. Some have subconsciously realised that their penetrating eyes cause discomfort so they tend to wear dark or tinted glasses, even indoors.

Hustlers often try to get some illusory advantage so that they may later demand a favour in return. One technique they use is to be too tactile by shaking hands, touching you or sitting very close in the hope that they will embarrass you and so gain some social advantage.

In conversation Hustlers soon give themselves away. They often tell stories about their contacts with celebrities. They tend to use first names early, both that of the person they are talking to and any name that they think will impress. Hustlers are name-droppers and social climbers so they pepper their conversation with the names of the latest restaurants, shows, people and so on. Their conversation is as smooth as a television talk show.

Another trait of the Hustler is to talk about money early in the conversation. Hustlers believe that making money is easy so this emphasis in conversation is not surprising. Hustlers also tend to be gamblers and love going to horse races, casinos and dog races. Anecdotes about their own gambling successes and others' failures crop up often in their conversation. Hustlers enjoy telling stories, particularly about incidents that present them in a favourable light.

Hustlers often tend to take a robust view of the law. They tend to go as close as they can to breaking it without doing so; for example, they always drive just over the speed limit. Hustlers will spend much time analysing rules so that they can bend them to their advantage. The irony is that if the reverse happens and a Hustler is caught out on some technicality then he or she will go on and on about other people's imperfections and lack of ethics.

Hustlers closely follow the letter of the law but often forget the spirit. This casuistic sense of morality causes them to tell you often, 'I am going to be perfectly honest with you.' When the Hustler says this you should be on your guard, especially when he or she then goes on to describe how someone else is going to break the rules or be deceptive. You should be careful not to be taken for a ride. Otherwise you may finish in the worst position of all for a salesperson — close second.

Because they are charming and affable, Hustlers make friends easily. Their friendships are sometimes short, however, because other people may become tired of their emphasis on material objects. Sometimes Hustlers with low Normal prove to be untrustworthy and they are often snobs. The streak of snobbery manifests itself particularly in restaurants and hotels where Hustlers tend to treat the staff as members of a lower class. Hustlers divide the world into winners and losers. Hustlers do not care what people whom they consider to be losers think about them.

Hustlers will fawn over and pander to anyone they think is

higher in status than themselves or perceive to be winners, especially if they think such actions will help them climb the social ladder. As a result Hustlers sometimes seem sycophantic in the presence of their superiors.

Hustlers often divorce as they have generally married for the wrong reasons. Typically the Hustler appeals to the future spouse's maternal or paternal instinct, rather than the marriage stemming from both people wanting to form a mutual partnership. The spouse gets a divorce when the Hustler either has an affair or is felt not to be contributing fairly to a relationship. The divorce proceedings are usually long and drawn out because Hustlers are good at shedding crocodile tears, circumventing any blame and eliciting sympathy.

Hustlers are good opportunists, charming and very conscious of money — especially other people's. If they are intelligent and have lots of self-control they become successful businesspeople.

Hustlers are common in the upper echelons of business and government. They often make good salespeople as they are good at ingratiating themselves with prospects and show finesse. Hustlers are often promoted, but they find it difficult to be first-level managers because the other staff perceive them as superficial and lacking in depth. The person who conceived the adage, 'Great salespeople make poor sales managers' probably had a Hustler in mind. Frustrated, the Hustler sometimes moves to a higher position with a competitor. Hustlers tend to give the most loyalty to themselves.

Hustlers are surprisingly common in selling situations because they often become decision makers. If you meet a prospect who appears glib and a bit of a wheeler-dealer, you probably have a Hustler. The Hustler will buy only from someone whom he considers is hard-headed and shrewd like himself. Furthermore, since the Hustler often bends the rules and is an opportunist, you must always remember to be careful and conscientious, especially when acting in a selling role.

Anti-Hustlers are most commonly found in either mass consumer markets or in service institutions such as hospitals or social welfare. They are the people who want to sacrifice themselves for others. They are uninterested in money; they are sometimes so over-generous that they become painful to their colleagues. Sometimes the deficiency is so great that the Anti-Hustler suffers from the martyr complex. An example of the martyr complex is the mother who centres all her interest on her children with the expectation of total support when the children reach maturity.

Other examples of Anti-Hustlers are employees who, after a long period of work, honestly believe that the company should completely support them, regardless of present performance. So, in a strange way, a person completely lacking in Hustler and a person totally dominated by it share the characteristic of believing that the world owes them a living.

Selling to a Hustler

If you were selling a car to a Hustler you would move him or her towards the bright red sporty vehicles, such as Ferraris and Porsches. You would stress the fact that only a few select individuals would have the class to own this car. You might also suggest that only today a special trade-in deal was available.

The Hustler divides the world up into winners and losers. The winners are a small group of people who are 'in-the-know', shrewd, opportunistic and have made it to the top by taking risks and manipulating other people whom they regard as weak and losers. Hustlers believe that the best way to achieve wealth is to use the techniques they learned as small children — charming comments, winning smiles and occasional emotional tantrums. Indeed much of the attraction of the Hustler is due to his or her childlike charm.

I will finish this chapter by quoting Fagin, from Charles Dickens' *Oliver Twist*, who is one of the great Hustlers of literature.

'Some conjurors say that number three is the magic number, and some say number seven. It's neither, my friend, neither. It's number one.'

THE NORMAL

IN the previous chapter we discussed the Hustler, who we said was driven by the desire for material success and possessed a childlike charm. As the Hustler is to the child so is the Normal to the adult. Normals are driven by the desire for social approval by their peers. To obtain this approval they must adjust their behaviour to conform with the expectations of their colleagues. The behaviour that Normals consider natural would be considered conformist by those lacking in Normal. Normals are concerned about ethics and consequently often work in professions such as law and accounting. We have chosen an accountant as the Normal stereotype in the cameo which follows. We have called our accountant Ms Penguin. This is because the black and white formality of the penguin so reflects the controlled nature of the Normal. Black, white and grey — particularly charcoal grey — are the colours of the Normal. Normal men and women often wear white shirts, charcoal grey suits and discreet jewellery or ties. Just as penguins gather in flocks, so do Normals, who prefer to work in large organisations which have standards, policies and traditions.

We have all met people with big Normals. Your parents and older relatives will usually be high Normals.

First Call on a Normal

D.M.G. Sanderson was one of the big ten accounting firms. Recently the professional body regulating the accountants had decided to allow advertising. I was an account executive for a local advertising agency (known as 'a suit' by the creative staff, all of whom wore baggy trousers and casual tops) and a telemarketing campaign had secured several appointments. I was to see Pauline Penguin, the partner responsible for administration.

I arrived at the office five minutes early. The offices were mahogany and had discreet grey carpets. The receptionist was conservatively dressed and had a beautifully modulated English accent. I was asked to sit down. On the table were the standard society journals and business magazines. Right on time a younger woman stepped into the foyer. She was in neat black suit and white shirt. She was wearing black court shoes, conservative jewellery and an expensive watch. Her hair was extremely well-groomed and her make-up was discreet.

'Jim Smith?' she said, extending her hand.

'Yes. Pauline Penguin, I presume.' We both laughed slightly as we shook hands.

'Thank you for coming in. I have arranged for some other people to meet with us. Come along to the board room.'

We proceeded down the hall to a room with a large boardroom table at which several people were sitting. They were all wearing blue pin-striped suits, white shirts and conservative ties except for one. He

The Normal

was wearing a grey suit, a pale blue shirt and a striped tie. The three blue pin-stripes were the senior audit, tax, and consulting partners while the grey suit was Mr Jones, a recently appointed public relations consultant.

After shaking hands and introducing ourselves we all sat down. We then handed around business cards.

'Just like the Japanese,' one of the partners commented.

We all gave a slight laugh.

'Well I guess it's my turn to be in the chair,' said Ms Penguin.

'I have had an agenda produced so I suppose we should begin with that. Here, everyone, have a copy.'

All of us studied the agenda.

'Any requests for changes? No? Well let's begin. Before I proceed however, I think I should inform you, Mr Smith, that every decision in this practice has to be one of total agreement among the four of us. We have asked Mr Jones along because he is an expert in this area and he has said it is important for promotional efforts to be coordinated.'

'Oh, I agree.'

'Yes, we thought the point had logical appeal.'

'Item one on the agenda is a brief introduction to our company. That onerous task falls on to me. Essentially D.M.G. Sanderson is one of the oldest audit practices in the world. We are not the biggest but we think we are the best. We are particularly good at hiring people from outside the company and, by a process of mutual interaction, developing new business areas. For example, our consulting division was the first in this city associated with an accounting firm and is still regarded as the best.

'We know little about advertising and it has been a matter of some debate at the last full partners' meeting whether we should spend hard-earned fees on advertising. However, it was agreed to appoint a subcommittee which you see here and we have been empowered to run a trial campaign on a restricted budget.'

'Well, I must agree that is logical.'

'Indeed. Suppose you tell us a little about your company. Do you have a company brochure?'

Profile of a Normal

If we compare the adult to the child we can think of several differences in behaviour. Children tend to cry or throw a tantrum when something goes wrong. Children tend to be far more emotional than adults and lack stability. As individuals mature they become more reserved and prudent. They desire social approval. Increasing age results in a more balanced personality, less likely to show emotional extremes. This change of personality as one becomes more mature and integrated into society is the development of the Normal component. The Normal component acts as a stabiliser on the other six components discussed so far. Some allusion to how self-control modifies these six components has already been made. For example:

- The over-excitable, distracting Mover changes into a friendly, sociable, enthusiastic optimist.
- The insecure, procrastinating Ditherer becomes a compassionate, cautious, conscientious and stable administrator.
- The detached, secretive Artist changes into a creative, imaginative, sensitive individual.
- The aggressive, arrogant Politician turns into a steadfast, decisive, forceful leader.
- The fussy, preoccupied Engineer becomes a thorough, meticulous and systematic project manager.
- The wheeler-dealer of the Hustler changes into the realistic, shrewd, astute acumen of the successful business executive.

If, as is common, the Normal is average to strong and combined with some other strong components then the individual is fortunate. The resulting combination is often a dynamic, powerful and integrated personality. The Normal both gives direction to and inhibits the other components.

The Normal acts as a veneer which society puts over the original personality of the individual. Normals tend to be people who follow the norms of the society in which they live. They observe the formal social courtesies; for example, they shake hands and exchange business cards early. They are punctual for appointments and dislike people who are late. They have tidy desks and have neat handwriting. They wear conservative clothes; for example a grey flannel suit of good quality is the uniform of the Normal man. At the start of a conversation the Normal appears reserved and inhibited.

Normals are calm and self-composed and appear to have a flat personality. Normals love to be part of a group and will use references to other people or precedents as supports for their arguments. They also prefer the use of logic to emotion — indeed if an emotional person is present Normals become uncomfortable.

Normals have a strong sense of morals; their conversation will be peppered with references to standards of conduct. The stereotype Normal is a professional such as a lawyer or accountant.

The Normal is sometimes perfectionist and dislikes finding mistakes in a proposal. Normals tend to call in experts and obtain group approval for an idea. Another characteristic of the Normal is the tendency to summarise at the end of a meeting and suggest an action plan.

The Normal, because of the desire for self-approval, acts as a modifier and a regulator of the other components. Normals also have other desires, such as a wish to improve themselves. The beneficiaries of this drive are the evening and part-time courses offered by various institutions and the how-to books sold in bookshops everywhere. The Normal practises persistently. The sport of the Normal is golf, which consists of learning an artificial swing and is dominated by individuals who practise incessantly. Top golfers typically regard themselves as players who display much self-control.

Normals like to consider themselves as self-reliant and self-disciplined. Normals prefer individuals who stand on their own feet and who show the same emotional control as themselves. They are persistent when facing difficulties and exude a quiet confidence. The stereotype English person is a good example of the Normal component. Normals tend to be uncomplaining when faced with physical difficulties and show a 'stiff upper lip'.

Along with their desire for social approval, Normals respect the social norms. Tact, social mindfulness and respect for the privacy of another individual are all manifestations of the Normal desire for social approval. A basic goodness and charity towards other people, tempered with the need to follow social conventions, pervades the Normal personality. It is not surprising that England and Switzerland, which are among the most Normal countries, have founded many of the world's charities and have been frequent originators of philanthropic and nursing organisations such as the Red Cross.

People who have high Normal without any other strong component appear as unbending, rigid conservatives. People often accuse high Normals of being cold and colourless. High Normals demand high standards from others and they believe in both the letter and the spirit of the law. Their demands for high standards usually extend to their children and the result is often a conflict between parent and child. The same problem can occur in companies where a rigid orthodoxy of behaviour alienates new employees and causes the radicals to leave early so that only the more conventional stay. An organisation must adapt to its environment to survive, so the loss of the people who are most likely to come up with creative solutions to problems of change can prove fatal. Strong Normals are self-reliant; in a perverse way this characteristic may lead to difficulties when solutions need to be obtained by a group.

Weak Normals have no control over any dominant component and the condition can lead to mental illness if associated with an extreme of one of the other six components. If no other component is dominant the weak Normal will appear unbalanced and uncontrolled. The conversation is often inconsistent and irrational and the individual is likely to break down under pressure. The Normal tends to increase as a person gets older but it may begin to weaken slowly as the individual approaches senility or 'second childhood'. If the Normal continues to weaken beyond the state of dotage, then madness may develop.

King Lear is a good example of the strong Normal at the beginning of the play. The Normal is so strong that he causes his daughter Cordelia to lose her inheritance for failing to follow a social convention. However, as the play progresses, the Normal slowly disintegrates and Lear gradually goes mad.

Selling to a Normal

It is common to find considerable Normal when selling to decision makers in large organisations. The Normal likes to feel part of a group. In the same way that a bank manager requires you to provide references before approving a loan, the Normal likes to have either organisations or experts who can provide references about your product. The best references of all are satisfied clients who have bought your product and are happy users. This explains why the reference sale is perhaps the most common and successful technique used in industrial selling. People with high Normal who buy the fleets of cars for large organisations are often influenced by the number of cars sold so far to independent organisations and individuals.

If you were trying to sell a car to a Normal you would use such phrases as:

'The design of this car is very *logical* . . .'

'We consider that this manufacturer maintains exceptional levels of *quality control* and *service training* . . .'

'Many of our more *discerning* customers have chosen this model.'

'In this world you *get what you pay for* . . .'

'*Everyone knows* this car is simply the best.'

A person with high Normal will tend to prefer cars that are esteemed for quality and have wide approval, such as Mercedes, Jaguars or Rolls Royces. They will generally choose colours such as white, black or grey.

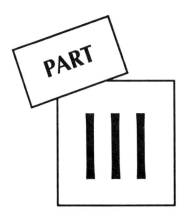

PART

III

EMPATHY
SELLING

CHAPTER 10
USING THE TECHNIQUE

TO the pragmatic salesperson the theory expounded in this book should be easy to learn and sufficiently sensitive to help meet the key objectives in selling: to quickly close a profitable sale and develop a long-term consultative relationship with your clients.

How does the theory help us? First it teaches us an important lesson of selling — the buyer is not the same as the salesperson. Many novice salespeople fail because they assume all prospects think and act the same — just like themselves. The assumption that people should think and act just like oneself is a common one; for example, those who are easily discouraged commonly expect others to be equally easily disheartened by every difficulty. Few people lose their subjectivity and develop the skill of analysing people objectively. As the analysis of the seven component types clearly shows, people are very different. They have differing goals and characteristics. The first benefit to salespeople of using the techniques of Empathy Selling is to lose their egocentricity.

Selling is an emotional process. Unless the buyer becomes emotionally involved in the proposition he or she will not usually buy. (One exception to this rule is when a buyer becomes so bored with the salesperson that he or she buys the product just to get rid of the salesperson!)

To trigger a buyer's emotions productively it is necessary to change one's own behaviour. This is the second important lesson of Empathy Selling. People have different ways of behaving and the secret of empathy is to adapt your own behaviour so that the prospect likes both you and your product.

Professional salespeople know you sell a product or service when it satisfies an emotional want of the prospect. A secret of sales success is to uncover the emotional want of the prospect and then satisfy it by tailoring the presentation of the product or service. The Empathy Selling technique allows you to uncover these wants quickly and accurately and to tailor your proposal accordingly.

Finally, much selling is based on developing a lasting relationship with the client. What makes an enduring business relationship thrive depends on many factors, such as product quality and service and professional and ethical standards. However, as in marriage, personality compatibility between the partners is a crucial factor. If that is missing, or if one partner does not adapt to the personality of the other, a divorce is often the result. Following the axiom: 'The customer is always right', the sales consultant who needs to develop long-term relationships with a number of clients will have to alter his or her behaviour to be consistently successful. Empathy Selling provides a basis for developing long-term relationships with clients.

Textbooks about selling seldom stress the emotionalism exhibited by prospects. Many books and films about selling are too idealistic. They tend to emphasise positive mental attitude and the need for structured selling techniques. While these are important, many of the examples quoted are imaginary and not typical of the real world.

In a typical textbook example the salesperson has an appointment, the secretary is friendly and the prospect invites the salesperson to his or her office for an amicable conversation. After a minute's gentle probing the salesman discovers that the prospect does not have any widgets. Widgets have been in existence for about five years and have a 100 per cent track record for quality and reliability. The three references quoted by the salesperson turn out to be the prospect's closest friends. Installing a widget will result in a cost-saving for the company equal to last year's net profit and because the salesperson's firm has patent protection, there is no competition for the next ten years. The salesperson asks if the prospect wants a blue or red widget, brings out this month's 10 per cent discount special offer, and the order is taken.

The reality is generally different. In an industrial service sale for a new product you are directed to talk to a technical purchasing officer. You spend the next three months writing at least six technical studies and proposals; each document is different and fifty pages long. After many broken appointments you finally meet the decision maker. The day before the meeting your head office announces a 20 per cent price rise with no exceptions. After the meeting has lasted ten minutes you realise that your main competitor has just provided the prospect with one year's free trial of their new product. Finally, after another ten minutes the prospect informs you that four years ago a salesperson from your firm offered a one-month free trial for a different product. The product never worked and your credit department, unaware of the free trial, sued the prospect for nonpayment.

If you are a real estate agent, how often do you meet a prospective buyer who enters holding a cheque from a lottery win? The prospect tells you that since their marriage he and his wife have wanted to live in Bay Street and they have just seen the house with your sign on it. You take the couple to see the house, counter the wife's objection to the neighbours by telling her they are emigrating and accept the deposit.

No, the reality is that your prospective buyers see about fifty houses over a period of six months and then ring you every week to ask if there is anything new. Suddenly, they ask about a house they inspected three months ago without a flicker of interest. When you tell them with some pride that you sold it last week, they suddenly become excited. Both then complain bitterly that you failed to tell them about the offer and refuse to speak to you again.

Few salespeople are fortunate enough to sell a new product with such a substantial advantage in price/performance that there is no effective competition. In most selling situations the competition is such that real differences among the products are marginal. Which product is chosen then depends on other factors such as the reputation of the supplying company and the empathy developed with the prospect by the salesperson. So in competitive selling — which is the selling that happens in the real world — Empathy Selling can turn out to be the competitive difference.

I am a strong believer in the 'KISS principle', which stands for 'Keep It Simple, Stupid!' Although I have read theoretical papers that expand the selling process into a complex web of interactions,

I prefer simplicity. As far as I am concerned a sale comprises four steps:

1 You try to establish whether the prospects have the authority to make a decision, need your product or service and have the money to pay for it.
2 If there is a need, you describe the benefits of your product in such a way that the prospects believe their needs will only be satisfied by its purchase.
3 You handle objections raised by the prospects or their associates.
4 You close the sale by getting a commitment from the prospects to purchase your product or service and become clients.

In the next four chapters we will discuss each of these four steps in detail:

• Qualifying the prospect;
• Tailoring the proposal;
• Handling objections;
• Closing the sale.

Once you have read these four chapters you should have a solid understanding of how to apply the techniques of Empathy Selling.

ANALYSING THE PROSPECT

O NE reason why Empathy Selling is easy to learn is that it only uses seven components. As this is the limit of short-term memory for most people it makes sense that any method of analysing the prospect should itself only use a maximum of seven steps.

It is even better if the seven steps can be summarised into a meaningful word or mnemonic, such as KISS above. Mnemonics are another secret of success in selling. The word is derived from the name of the Greek goddess of memory and is defined as something that helps the memory. The technique is to form an acronym from the first letters of the words of the various steps. People have used acronyms throughout history; RADAR, for example, stands for **Ra**dio **De**tecting **A**nd **R**anging.

In the following sections mnemonics are used extensively. Keith Stevenson first summarised many of them in his highly recommended sales anthology, *Go Selling*.

The first letters of the component types, NHMDAPE, unfortunately do not form a mnemonic, but the steps for type analysis do: it is 'TOPDOG'.

These letters stand for the following component clues:

T Talk
O Organisation
P Position
D Dress
O Office
G Gambit

Remember this mnemonic and you will become the topdog sales executive in your organisation. Each of these six clues will now be examined to see how they help determine the dominant components in a prospect's personality.

Analysing the prospect

Talk

Both the manner and content of a prospect's conversation provide useful indications of the dominant personality components.

We will see in Chapter 18 how Empathy Selling uses the work of Bandler and Grindler in Neuro-Linguistic Programming (NLP) and Donald Moine's theories of modern persuasion techniques. The basic thesis of NLP is that people accept data primarily from three senses: sight, hearing and touch. Furthermore, individuals tend to prefer one channel and, as a result of conditioning, their preferred sense can be detected in the way they talk, their eyes and their gestures.

Visual people use sight words such as *see*, *imagine* and *picture*. They rub or point to their eyes or glasses and their eyes tend to defocus when they are thinking or imagining.

Auditory people use words such as *listen*, *sound* and *communicate*. They tend to touch their chins or ears and move their eyes from side to side.

The kinaesthetic people use words such as *feel*, *sense* and *support*. They tend to rub their hands together or cross their arms over their chest and heart.

These three types correspond to the Artist, the Politician and the Engineer. Engineers, for example, tend to have monotonous voices and be boring conversationalists. They tend to use feeling words; for example:

'I am sure the board will be *cold* on the idea.'

'Just because you have had some *soft touches* before don't think you can *twist* a hard-headed company like ours.'

'You will have to let us *handle* the proposal in our own way and in our own time.'

'My spouse will have to be *warm* on the idea before we make a decision.'

When drunk, Engineers become pedantic and trying. They are often opinionated but are able to change their minds.

Politicians are also opinionated but they rarely change their minds. Their prejudices often appear in conversation. Politicians refer to themselves constantly, and their conversations are usually articulate and argumentative.

They tend to use sound words in their conversation; for example:

'*Tell* me about your company.'

'Please *amplify* that point.'

'That *sounds* interesting. Have you any independent reports?'

'My spouse will have to *hear* you before we make a decision.'

The third of the introvert components, the Artists, rarely refer to themselves. They are tight-lipped about themselves and their families. Compared with the tiger-like Politicians, Artists are like clams, as we have seen. Artists sometimes have speech impediments and many of them talk with their hands over their faces, with thumb and index finger pointing to the eyes.

The conversation of the Artist is punctuated with sight words; for example:

'Have you got a *picture* of the product?'

'I can't *imagine* we would ever use it.'

'My spouse will have to *see* you before we make a decision.'

Many people believe Artists to be cold, snooty and indifferent when, in reality, they are just shy. All three of the introvert components share a degree of formality and it takes some time for them to use first names.

On the other hand the three extrovert components all tend to use first names straight away. Ditherers appear submissive and love to socialise. They are complainers, imagining either that there is something wrong with themselves or their families or that a disaster is going to strike the organisation for which they work. They love to listen to other people's problems and when listening to a tale of woe they cheer up immensely.

Movers are the opposite. They have big, beaming smiles and they talk quickly and enthusiastically. They often appear to be highly strung and fidgety because they tend to gesticulate and jump about in conversation from one topic to another. They also love to socialise. Unlike the Ditherer, who worries about trifles, the Mover prefers the big picture and hates to be bogged down in detail.

Hustlers also move quickly in conversation to a first-name basis. They are name droppers and egocentrics and tend to stretch the truth. Hustlers have a limited sense of morality but spend much time talking about the letter of the law and how people try to evade it. Their conversation also tends to include money and gambling.

Normals appear cold and composed in conversation. They tend to argue logically and rarely become emotional. They observe formal social courtesies such as shaking hands and exchanging cards.

Organisation

Organisations, as well as individuals, develop behavioural characteristics which decide their success in the business environment. For each type of industry it is possible to suggest components which will lead to organisational growth and development. These components will tend to become norms of behaviour. Norms refer to the standard of behaviour that is derived from the expectations of people both inside and outside the organisation. Good examples are such comments as 'X is a creative advertising agency' or 'Z is a marketing company'. People who have the expected norm as their dominant components will tend to succeed in those organisations. Each of the seven components can lead to success, depending on the organisation.

- The Normal component, with its emphasis on logic and precedent, tends to dominate professional organisations such as legal and accounting firms. Thus the people who staff these organisations tend to be either high Normals or Hustlers who have mimicked the Normal component.
- Hustlers are agents. Their ability to tell both sides of a story helps in such fields as stockbroking, merchant banking, real estate, car dealerships and so on. Only individuals with considerable Hustler can handle both buyers and sellers quickly and profitably.
- The Mover works best in service industries which deal with numbers of people, such as retailing and fast foods. The enthusiasm and energy of Movers make them excellent employees and, later, managers in these industries.
- Ditherers are preoccupied with security. Suitable industries include those concerned with potential disasters, such as insurance or transport monopolies.
- Artists are creative, iconoclastic yet withdrawn. They are found in industries where creativity is critical to success, such as advertising and fashion.
- Politician norms of behaviour tend to be followed in bureaucracies and big companies. Position, office size and status symbols are some manifestations of this component. It is also common in the largest company within an industry.
- Engineers tend to dominate building design companies and consultants, where the work flow tends to be a succession of projects. To succeed in an Engineering organisation you have to be successful at planning and completing projects.

If you are unsure about the norms of a company, look at its annual report. It is unnecessary to look inside or calculate any financial ratios, just examine the cover. If it is bright and flashy it is probably a Hustler organisation. If it contains many photographs of people it is probably a Mover company. A subtle and creative touch suggests an Artist company.

Although you should never take these first suggestions about personality type as the final determinant (the clues discussed below are probably more important), understanding the norms of an organisation can be most useful, particularly for large capital goods or service sales. Slanting the proposal towards the dominant goal of an organisation can be effective, especially if you need to prepare a written proposal that will be considered by the board.

Position

Just as organisations may have dominant components, so too do certain positions or functions.

Successful General Managers, who need logic, ceaseless energy and a thirst for success, tend to be a combination of Normal, Mover and Politician.

Marketing people generally succeed if they are emotional and have lots of enthusiasm and a manipulative streak. Thus marketing personnel tend to be low in Normal, and high in Mover and Hustler.

Administrative staff require the ability to double-check and do monotonous and detailed work, and so tend to combine strong Normal and Ditherer components.

Personnel staff need to be able to meet a number of people during the day for interviews and other meetings so generally have high Mover component. On the other hand they need to be sensitive so need high Artist.

Electronic Data Processing (EDP) managers generally come from software backgrounds which tend to hire people with a lot of Ditherer (to check the code) and Engineer (to complete the project). To rise above the ruck the individual needs a lot of Politician as well. Hence EDP managers tend to reflect their initials.

Besides the position in an organisation, another useful clue is a manager's secretary. Since like attracts like, managers often select staff who have similar components to their own.

Dress

Dress and general appearance are key signals of personality. The fashion industry bases its appeal on the assumption that clothes and appearance are a reflection of the personality. 'The apparel oft proclaims the man' or, the modern equivalent, 'I dress to make a statement about myself'.

It is most important when selling to recognise the Hustler. This can be difficult as Hustlers are able to mimic other personality types and go undercover; however, the dress of the Hustler provides important clues. As discussed earlier, the clothes are generally glitzy, if not flashy. For example male Hustlers often wear red or orange striped ties and both males and females often wear ostentatious watches and bracelets. Female Hustlers will have rings on at least two or three fingers and heavy gold earrings. Their casual clothes are often open-necked to show off gold chains and necklaces. Another clue which we have noted earlier is that Hustlers often wear designer label clothes as they love to drop names.

Normals tend to wear high quality, conservative clothes in sober colours such as grey. The men's ties tend to be conservative and often show some form of repetitive emblem representing a club, school or university.

Ditherers tend to choose higher quality clothes, too, as they believe cheap clothes are poor buys because they will soon fall apart. As the Ditherer male has an overpowering need for security he too wears club ties. He usually has a short back and sides haircut. There is a Mother Earth colouring about Ditherers' clothes; browns and greens tend to dominate. Ditherer women tend to have big handbags filled with all sorts of make-up and other items as a precaution against any unforeseen eventuality.

As we saw in Chapter 5, Artists tend to wear very imaginative clothes and be in the forefront of fashion. The ties of the men and the dress of the women often contain unusual patterns. The men usually have beards and both sexes tend to avoid eye contact.

Movers and Engineers tend to have a tousled appearance. Movers usually have their coats off, collars unbuttoned and sleeves rolled up. They often appear to be rushing from one task to another. They like to wear casual clothes such as jeans, running shoes and loose-fitting shirts and pullovers. Movers like bright colours and patterns. They often have a message on their clothes such as 'Don't Worry — Be Happy', either in the form of a button, or emblazoned on the chest or back.

Engineers get very wound up in their work and so their shirts slip out of their trousers or skirts and their ties work loose without being noticed. The model Engineer is the absent-minded professor who puts on an unmatched pair of socks. Engineers like to carry around the tools of their trade, too, and often have pens in their shirt pockets or a Swiss knife on a belt. Female engineers often have something useful hanging around their neck such as a fob watch or a ballpoint pen. Both sexes often wear striped shirts which are in non-classic colours or patterns.

Office

No comment was made about the Politician's mode of dressing as it tends to be conventional and nondescript. It is the offices of Politicians which give them away. They are often in the most dominant position in the building and larger than the surrounding offices. Even if the offices are the same size the Politician's office contains status symbols such as name plates, degrees and certificates on the walls. Politicians generally place their desks in a dominant position. Both Politicians and Hustlers try to have entertaining areas if it is at all possible.

By contrast the office of the Artist often has the desk facing away from a view or window, as we have seen. The office furniture and lighting is typically of a modern, creative design. The desk is sometimes untidy as the Artist detaches himself from reality. Some form of original creative art often hangs on the wall.

The Hustler, on the other hand, often has a flashy reproduction on the wall and flamboyant decor. Because Hustlers are often divorced, as we discussed in Chapter 8, you will often see a family picture with the ex-wife missing.

Ditherers tend to have pictures of their families in a prominent position on their desks but in their case the whole family is in the photograph. As we saw in Chapter 4, they often have full ash-trays, as they are often compulsive smokers. They also cram their offices with files because they cannot bear to throw anything away and must keep a copy of everything just in case.

As noted in Chapter 7, Engineers often have timetables, project charts and pictures of big projects such as bridges, buildings or aeroplanes hanging on the wall. They usually have shelves crammed with books on a number of diverse topics. Their desks are usually untidy but they tend to know where everything is.

Movers also have untidy desks cluttered with the working papers of several simultaneous projects.

Normals are usually neat and tidy in their work and so have neat and tidy desks, situated in a neat and tidy office.

Gambit

A gambit is a term taken from chess which describes the first tactics made by a player to gain strategic advantage. In the same way, the gambit in a sales presentation describes the first manoeuvres made by the prospect. The first two moves usually made by prospects are:

- Being punctual for the meeting or not;
- Beginning with either a formal or informal mode of address.

Movers and Politicians will typically keep you waiting. Movers are late because they are always trying to do too many tasks at once and are always being distracted. Politicians are late because they subconsciously believe that by keeping the other person waiting they establish some form of superiority. The differences between the two are soon recognised. The Mover will arrive out of breath, apologise profusely, smile and start calling you by your first name. Politicians, on the other hand, will usually send down a secretary, keep you waiting again outside their office, make no apology and appear aloof and formal.

Punctual people tend to be Normals, Hustlers and Artists.

Normals tend to be punctual because time is money and punctuality is a socially approved habit. Hustlers arrive on time because they believe only losers are late. Being late also means that those who arrive on time may have gained additional information or a psychological advantage. Artists are punctual because they are sensitive to other people's feelings and would hate to keep anyone waiting. Normals will follow the social courtesies, shaking hands and exchanging cards. Artists will refrain from shaking hands and avoid eye contact. Hustlers will be friendly, shake hands and soon be on first name terms.

Engineers are usually hypocritical about punctuality. They hate being kept waiting but are often late for appointments themselves because they become preoccupied with their present project and lose track of time.

Ditherers are unusual in that they are never on time — they are either early or late. Ditherers sometimes arrive especially early because they are scared of being late and missing something important. On the other hand, if you are going somewhere with Ditherers for a meeting they will often make you late as they tend to fuss about checking their dress, what they need to take, accepting phone calls and so forth.

Conclusion

In summary the analysis of a prospect can be easily carried out using the TOPDOG mnemonic. In chapter 17 a simple checklist has been provided as an aid to component recognition. A useful exercise is to grade yourself and one or two close friends and then have them do the same to you. Below is a simple table that summarises the TOPDOG mnemonic across the seven personality components.

Once you have analysed a prospect the fun begins. Now you can tailor your proposal to the dominant components. If you have correctly picked the two or three dominant components you should be able to gain empathy with the client. You should be able to trigger the emotional 'hot buttons' and establish the positive rapport essential for closing the sale and developing a good long-term client relationship.

The TOPDOG Mnemonic

	Normal	Hustler	Mover	Ditherer	Artist	Politician	Engineer
Talk	logical	money	lively	hypochondriac	bashful	opinionated	monotonic
Organisation	professional	wholesale	retail	insurance	design	large	consultant
Position	administration	sales	sales	administration	creative executive	manager	project manager
Dress	conservative	flashy	tousled	earth colours	creative	conventional	pens in pocket
Office	neat	glitzy	messy	filled with files	oil painting	degrees	project plans
Gambit	on time, formal	on time, informal	late, informal	early or late	on time, formal	late, formal	on time, informal

CHAPTER 12
ADAPTING THE PROPOSAL

T HE first stage of a sales presentation is spent in establishing whether you are talking to the right person or the right man. This process is called prospect qualification. MAN is another useful mnemonic which was invented in more chauvinistic times. I apologise to all female readers but after much thought I was not able to come up with a less sexist substitute. The right MAN is an individual who fulfils the following three criteria:

- He or she has the Money to pay for your product or service if he or she decides to become a client. No money — no sale — no commission.
- He or she has the Authority to decide whether to use your product or service. If you are not talking to the decision maker you cannot get a decision.
- He or she has a perceived Need for your product or service.

Unless the prospect fulfils the three criteria of Money, Authority and Need then you may be trying to sell what has been aptly described as a china egg. A china egg is a prospect who never breaks, no matter how hard you try. The professional salesperson will aim at quickly winding up the presentation to a china egg while extracting as much information as possible about the organisation structure, other leads, needs for other services and so on.

A benefit of using the MAN mnemonic is that it provides you with time to establish the dominant components of the prospect's personality. Let us assume that you believe you have a genuine prospect and you have decided on the dominant personality components. What is now needed is a way of adapting your proposal and presentation method so that the prospect becomes a client.

The technique is simple; you adapt your proposal and presentation to fulfil the prospect's emotional wants. How this is done for each component is discussed in the following sections.

Adapting to a Normal

The sale to the Normal raises an issue that salespeople often debate. Should they admit directly that they are in sales or should they use other words such as 'account executive' or 'marketing consultant' to describe their position on their business cards? Many salespeople (particularly those dominated by the Hustler) try to disguise their job by describing themselves as consultants or account executives when they introduce themselves. Normals become uncomfortable with this deception when they realise they are talking to a salesperson and may then emotionally block further progress.

Another issue is how soon should sales executives present their business cards and how soon should they use brochures? When dealing with a Normal the answer is the sooner the better. If the Normal prospect does not receive a business card and brochures, then he or she unconsciously feels that something is lacking and that the salesperson is not following the accepted conventions.

The keys to selling to the Normal are references and logic. Normals want to feel part of a group and if you have client references or expert reports, especially from organisations and people with whom the prospect would be familiar, then you should use these aids again and again. It is because the Normal is so prevalent in our society that the reference sale is the most popular technique. The first question that many people ask when first confronted with a new product or service is 'Who else is using it?' If you have three or four well-known reference sales the question is easily answered. If not, it is a problem. A saying often quoted in the computer industry is that you can't get your first sale until you have your first installation; but you can't get your first installation until you have your first sale.

As the Normal has the goals of self-discipline and self-improvement, you should also stress how the adoption of your proposal will improve the standards and working methods of the buyer, be it an individual or an organisation.

The proposal should contain such phrases as 'better personal habits', 'increased leisure time', 'domestic order and tranquillity', 'improved working practices', 'increased order in the department', and 'co-ordinated work flow'. The other theme of the proposal should be how logical it is. Normals prefer logic to emotion. While I admit that it seems ironic in a book about emotional selling techniques to suggest logic as the first technique, it is the exception that proves the rule. The Normal is generally uncomfortable with an emotional presentation and perceives it as a hard sell.

Another excellent technique with Normals is to ask them to elaborate on a previous buying decision. For example, if a prospect who appears to have a high Normal component walks into a showroom, ask what car the prospect now drives and why did he or she buy it?

A sales representative for a cosmetic company could use a question such as:

'What did you look for when you last chose a facial cream?'

In industrial sales good questions would be:

'What are the decision-making criteria for capital equipment?'

'Does your company have a two-supplier policy?'

Some writers on selling techniques (for example Moine and Herd) call this the 'instant replay technique'. It is valuable with any prospect as it provides clues about an individual's personality and preferences; however it is particularly powerful for the Normal. By going over a previous buying decision and establishing both the buying motives and the order in which they appeared, the Normal prospect is generating an internal reference sale. It is a reference sale which the prospect knows and finds credible. The sales executive should remember that 87 per cent of people prefer to buy rather than be sold.

Adapting to a Hustler

Hustlers perceive themselves as part of a small minority of people who are shrewd opportunists. It has been said that there are two types of people in this world, those who divide the world into two classes and those who do not. The Hustler divides the world into winners and losers. If Hustlers consider that the salesperson they are dealing with is a winner they may buy on the salesperson's terms. Hustlers buy from losers on their own terms, generally after they think they have extracted the last cent of discount. Thus the first step towards making profitable sales to Hustlers is to convince them that you are a winner.

To make the Hustler see you as a winner you must first look like one, and here considerations such as dress, manner and voice are all important. Your dress should be neat, expensive and impressive. Your manner should be superior and your speech confident. When the Hustler tells you about meeting your Managing Director last mo..th, reply with an account of your last meeting, or if that is impossible, relate some anecdote about your MD. The Hustler often exaggerates to impress so there is no reason why you should not take the same liberty. Hustlers do not usually mind you exaggerating; it is only when a misrepresentation causes them to lose money that they become bitter. If you are able to uncover some mistake or minor deceit while you are talking, pull up a Hustler immediately. Hustlers do not worry about being caught out and you will go up in their estimation as a result. If you overlook Hustlers' falsehoods they will consider you weak and think they are successfully pulling the wool over your eyes.

Do not be afraid to talk money early with Hustlers. They usually bring up finance issues early themselves. Hustlers will buy only if they think they are getting a better deal than anyone else and there are two ways that you can convince them they are. One is to give them a special deal — if not in price, then in some way that does not cost your company much but is perceived as valuable by the customer. One classic technique is to offer a 'special' guarantee that is part of your company's standard terms and conditions. Another is to create an artificial discount. The easiest way is to lift your standard prices by say 25 per cent and then be forced to offer 15 per cent off. Hustlers will then demand something more so you let them squeeze another 5 per cent off. Both of you are then happy — you have sold at 5 per cent over the standard book price and the Hustler has negotiated a 20 per cent discount.

When describing the benefits of your product, stress any

immediate and personal gains, as the Hustler usually takes a short-term view of the world. If introducing the product helps make the Hustler more visible in the organisation and will therefore help his or her image, say so. The Hustler is a vain person and appeals to the ego work wonders. Another technique is to show how the product will help the Hustler move up into higher social groups. The Hustler is a potential socialite and will embrace such suggestions with relish. Hustlers are the only types you should wine and dine, particularly at the latest fashionable restaurants. You should arrange to get the best table and tell the headwaiter to refer to both you and your client by last names and speak to you as an old and valued customer. The promise of a large tip to the waiter is all that is necessary. This treatment appeals to the Hustler who will go around for days afterwards talking about it.

My final advice for dealing with Hustlers is to take everything they say with a pinch of salt and, when selling, try to tie them down with legally binding documents as quickly as possible.

Adapting to a Mover

Selling to the Mover is easy; just remember to 'Smile, smile, smile'! If you are enthusiastic, the Mover will respond with even more enthusiasm. In complete contrast to selling to a Normal, you should forget logic and use as much emotion as possible. It is also important to remember that the Mover is easily distracted and finds it difficult to concentrate. You should therefore disregard details as the Mover prefers to deal with general concepts. When confronted with a Mover, novice salespeople often fall into the trap of giving a longwinded monologue of product features. This is because the Mover appears to react enthusiastically to every new feature or benefit raised, so the salesperson, in turn, enthusiastically moves on to the next feature instead of closing.

A technique which works well with all individuals but best of all with Movers and Ditherers is the 'repeated yes technique'. In its simplest form this technique consists of asking a series of questions to which you expect affirmative answers. The most famous example is the cold canvassing for an appointment, by telephone.

'Hello. Is this Ms Jackson?
'Yes, it is.'
'You live at 27 Raglan Street, East Riding?'
'Yes, I do.'
'Do you have a vacuum cleaner?'
'Yes, of course.'
'Do you occasionally have difficulty removing stubborn stains caused by mud or spilt liquids?'

and so on.

The Mover likes agreement and everyone being happy and sociable. The repeated yes is an excellent way of generating empathy. Good questions to ask are:

'Would it be fair to say . . .?'
'Do you sometimes feel . . .?'
'Have you ever seen something like this before?'

Another way of generating repeated yes answers is to end each instruction during a demonstration with 'OK', 'all right', or simple questions; for example:

'Push this button here, OK?'
'Call this number if you need further assistance, all right?'
'Then you twist the button on the right to the left. Are you following me?'

Since the Mover is so sociable, you should stress the group benefits of the product. In contrast to the Hustler it is the social benefits of a product or service which appeal to the Mover. Another good sales technique with Movers is to ask for the organisation chart of the prospect and slowly go through it, establishing benefits for as many departments as possible. If you are selling a domestic product or service, try to establish a benefit for each member of the family.

It is also a good technique to introduce Movers to as many members of your organisation as possible. The Mover is happiest visiting outside offices and inspecting reference sites. If you can engender a feeling of team-work then you will maximise the likelihood of the sale. Once you have established some key benefits, keep repeating them. Movers are so easily distracted that they soon forget the benefits of your product and you as well. Keep beaming back and you will usually get a warm reception from the Mover. If you fail to close at the first sales call, keep contacting the Mover every day. Otherwise the Mover will forget you as soon as a competitor appears and try to please the new salesperson.

Adapting to a Ditherer

Ditherers are dissatisfied with their lot in life but are too insecure to change it. The first point when selling to a Ditherer is to remember that it will be a long sale. You should consider whether it is cost-effective to sell to Ditherers at all; however, you should also remember that once the Ditherer is a client it will take much effort from your competitors to persuade him or her to change suppliers. Hence Ditherers generally make excellent reference sales. When asked for a reference they will first begin by criticising some features of your product or service but then go on to say how your product is the best on the market and they will never change. The initial criticism does not harm your reputation but gives it credibility because all buyers know that no product or service is perfect.

The first step when selling to a Ditherer is to ask him or her for a criticism of the present product or service. Fear not, a series of criticisms will follow, punctuated with sighs, groans and whimpers.

During the litany use the repeated yes technique to generate agreement. There are two particular methods which work well with the Ditherer. One is to repeat back what the customer says in a question form that requires a yes answer; for example:

'Because you now have children you need a larger oven and more kitchen storage space?'
'You want to wear a dress to the school cocktail party that is not black?'

The other method is to convert generalities into questions.

'Quality has declined for many products, hasn't it?'
'Levels of service have declined in many industries, haven't they?'

About an hour later, when the Ditherer has finished, you should have enough material to suggest various avenues of approach. Whatever approach you then choose, stick to it, go slowly and be clear with each selling proposition. Ditherers become confused easily and are sometimes slow on the uptake. Alternatives will slow them down. A good approach is to use direct questions or 'tie-downs' that gradually narrow their range of choice. The Ditherer will ask many 'What if?' questions and it is important not to be impatient. Your answers should be as simple and explicit as possible.

In your proposal you should stress the quality of your company's product or service and the improbability of any defect to try to overcome any insecurity. Another method to overcome fear and doubt is to use reference sells. You should also show how simple the product is to use. One common method is to arrange a hands-on demonstration. Another is to jointly plan how to carry out the first steps of introducing the product or service.

Use the instant replay technique. If possible you should try to discover any previous times when the Ditherer prospect successfully introduced a change in the organisation and use these incidents to boost confidence in your own company's product or service.

Ditherers usually have stable job histories. Even though they are loyal employees they sometimes develop a reputation as complainers. Nevertheless at one time or another they will have been asked to undertake some change for their company. Because they are so cautious and prone to double checking, they will usually have been successful in implementing the change.

The salesperson should aim at counteracting the gloom of the Ditherer with optimism. As stated earlier, the Mover and Ditherer are the emotional components and there tends to be a cycle between the Mover and Ditherer. If you are having a return meeting with a Ditherer try to make it on a Monday morning. As we saw in Chapter 4, after a weekend at home the Ditherer will often approach the office enthusiastically because it represents a change of environment.

Adapting to an Artist

The shy, sensitive Artist is another type who needs a long, soft sell. Repeated calls will be needed but again, once sold, Artists should prove to be loyal clients. Artists loathe the hard sell so you should use soft-selling methods such as jointly arriving at a solution, avoiding eye contact and slowing down your rate of speech.

If the Artist perceives you as glib and insincere the chances of a successful sale are slim. Because Artists dislike social contact and think of themselves as individuals, you should aim at having several short person-to-person meetings rather than one long heavy presentation.

A good sales technique is to appeal to the Artist's imagination. Begin any presentation by giving a history of the product and your organisation. Go into some detail and throughout the story ask the Artist to imagine what was happening.

Use pictures. The good salesperson should have some sales aids containing pictures or diagrams and Artists will prefer to consider them rather than suffer a series of questions. If you find that they are good at drawing, get them to sketch out some ideas on paper. Be careful, however, of suggesting this in front of other people as it might cause embarrassment. Otherwise use a white board or pad to make points and images.

Use visual words. Among some of the more useful visual words are:

Clear: Have I been clear on how you would use this product or do you want me to explain something further?

Examine: Let's examine how you would use this in your home.

Focus: Focus in on this feature — you will soon recognise how it provides this key benefit.

Imagine: Imagine how your staff will like this.

Look: Look at the quality of this cloth.

Picture: Have you got a picture in your mind about how this will work?

View: Do you imagine your board will view this proposal favourably?

Other useful words are *observe, see, survey, watch* and *well-defined.*

As with the Ditherer, try to find out successful decisions the Artist has made. Adapt the instant replay technique by showing the Artist how to reapply the creativity used in those earlier decisions. Most important, you should ask the Artist to imagine how he or she or the organisations would use the product or service you are selling. You should not labour the detail during presentations to Artists as they are usually quick to perceive relationships. On the other hand, you should ask direct instead of indirect questions. Artists can imagine so many sides to a question and are so sensitive about offending anyone with their answers that they often provide vague replies to indirect questions. In the first stages of a presentation to an Artist, you should be careful not to force the prospect to take an entrenched position. It is difficult to change Artists' minds and they can prove to be most stubborn.

In conclusion, the Artist requires a soft sell, a stress on the product features, the use of visual words and continuous appeals to the imagination.

When presenting to an A avoid eye contact and do not cause embarrassment.

Adapting to a Politician

The complementary component to the Artist, the Politician can be equally stubborn and will often refuse to change an opinion once it is given. Thus, if you are trying to get a Politician to change suppliers, you should never first ask the Politician if the company is happy with its present supplier. Politicians are reluctant to change their opinions, no matter how forceful or logical the argument. This is in contrast to the Ditherer who, if you ask if the company is satisfied with a present supplier, will dredge up small incidents of dispute that happened five years ago.

The technique with the Politician is to sow the seeds and let them germinate. The best method is to use examples of large organisations as reference sells. Give them the telephone numbers of two or three large organisations and let them ring up and listen to what your references say. Another technique is to quote from articles in well-known magazines. For the Politician, 'big is best'. If you can arrange meetings with important people, so much the better.

If you can, try to establish some way in which the purchase of the product will draw attention to the Politician. For instance, if a proposal has to go to the board, use the Politician's name on the front page of the proposal and, if possible, sprinkle it throughout the document. Another method is to show how the use of your product will make the Politician and the company the leaders in their country, if not the world.

As the Politician is opinionated and dogmatic you are bound to have differences. Politicians like people who stand up to them — it proves that they share with the Politician the key characteristic of backbone. So you must stand up to the Politician when needed. However you should be tactful and avoid putting the Politician on the defensive.

Ask Politicians for their opinions and suggest you need their help. Their egos make them unable to stop themselves from helping you. Another technique is to find out where your opinions concur and then widen the area of common agreement.

You achieve this commonality by asking indirect questions. Instead of 'How many times has your courier service been late?', ask 'In your opinion, what are the criteria that should be used in choosing a courier service?' Politicians love to answer indirect questions and to give opinions. The other problem with direct questions is that they may make the Politician seem ignorant — this is disastrous and nothing will engender antagonism more quickly.

Talk with auditory words. Among the more useful are:

Hear: Do you hear what I am saying?

Listen: Listen carefully. This next part of our conversation is important.

Quiet: We describe our service people as the quiet achievers.

Report: This reference report from one of the top twenty companies amplifies what I have been telling you.

Sound: How does this service sound to you so far?

Tell: Doesn't the quality of this cloth tell you something?

Talk: Have you heard anyone talk about this product before?

If you do have an argument with a Politician and it begins to get heated, suggest that you leave and come back later. This 'another meeting' technique works well and will usually defuse the crisis. Politicians have arguments all the time. They soon forget any argument once it has been resolved and finish by referring to it as a minor disagreement. It is unresolved conflicts which lead to grudges. Politicians, although trying, are usually good prospects. Of all the component types they are the most likely to make a quick decision. If you appeal to their need for status and prestige and use auditory words you should obtain favourable results.

Adapting to an Engineer

Once recognised, the Engineer is another relatively easy, if protracted, sale. The goal in life for the Engineer is to complete inspired projects. Make introducing your product or service an inspired project and you increase your chances of success. You need to remember that the Engineer is probably already working on another inspired project. So your first selling task is to work out the current timetable of projects and put the introduction of your product at the top of the list. This is most easily done by asking about the Engineer's present list of projects and establishing when the one he or she is currently working on will be finished. Suggest that when this project finishes the logical step would be to spend two or three days establishing priorities. You should then try to make an appointment. Do not make the appointment for an earlier date — the Engineer finishes projects on time. But make sure you have an appointment — Engineers become irritated if interrupted or distracted from their current task. Throughout the presentation stress the dominant benefit of your product and how it is useful.

You will have to go into detail — the Engineer is the technical buyer. You should try to provide as much detail as possible in the form of brochures or manuals. I once supplied to a prospect every technical manual on one computer range that I could before I got the sale. It needed six visits of ten minutes each. Every meeting was the same; I would first collect the three 200-page manuals that I had left behind at the last meeting, try to answer one or two questions and then hand over another three manuals. My only worry was that the computer would be obsolete before the prospect had completed all his reading. Engineers are bookworms and you should flood them with information about your product.

When presenting to the Engineer go slowly and word your proposal in terms of a 'plan', 'task' or 'project'. Engineers prefer thoroughness and attention to detail. They can be exhaustive in their questions so you should prepare for long meetings.

Use action-feeling words during presentations. Good examples of such words are:

Feel: How do you think your spouse will feel about it?

Grasp: Have you grasped the concept behind the product?

Handle: How do your staff currently handle this problem?

Hold: Hold everything — the answer has slipped my mind.

Respond: How will your board respond to this proposal?

Stress: I must stress how useful this product can be.

Touch: Touch this cloth and feel the quality.

Another good set of words are the temperature words:

'Are you (*hot, cold* or *lukewarm*) on the product?'

If you do not know the answer to a question, do not say, 'I don't know but I will get back to you later'. Use a different approach — hand over the manual and suggest that the Engineer finds the answer.

Engineers prefer to handle or touch the product, so a trial run or demonstration in which they use the product themselves is generally a good way of clinching a sale. They do not feel confident unless they have touched or operated the product. If you cannot organise a hands-on demonstration then, as a last resort, use other customers as references and describe how they used or responded to the product.

Conclusion

Many of the methods and selling techniques described above are familiar to most salespeople. Empathy Selling is different because it suggests that the success of a technique depends on the personality type of the decision-maker. For example, reference selling is used widely but, as you should now realise, reference sales appeal mainly to Normals, Ditherers and Politicians (if the reference sale is a big company). Artists and Engineers would most likely remain indifferent to reference selling and other strategies are needed.

Empathy Selling stops you as a salesperson from getting into a rut (once described as a grave with the ends kicked out). Instead of delivering the same presentation to all, you should now realise how you use different techniques for different personality types. The skill in Empathy Selling consists of first analysing your prospect and then adopting the appropriate techniques to maximise the likelihood of success. Using Empathy Selling will enable you to better understand your client's needs and wants and choose the best solutions for the individual from your company's range of products and services. You both end up in a win-win situation and should go on to develop a fruitful relationship.

*H*ANDLING OBJECTIONS

OBJECTIONS are part and parcel of selling. When novice salespeople start selling they meet objections to their product, their company or themselves. Empathy Selling is useful because it helps salespeople to anticipate objections and suggests ways of dealing with them. If you exclude imaginary or unfounded objections then there are seven basic objections salespeople often encounter when giving a presentation. (Again we obey the rule of having no more than seven items in a list.) The seven basic objections are:

1 Price.
2 Loyalty to an existing supplier.
3 I will not make a decision now.
4 Bad past experience with your company.
5 I do not like your company.
6 I do not like you.
7 Your proposition is not good enough.

In this chapter we shall consider each of these objections and learn how a knowledge of personality types helps us handle them.

Price

Two types will regularly bring up price as an objection — the Hustler and the Normal. The Hustler will usually ask the price of the product early in the sales presentation. If it is at all possible

IT IS NOT OUR COMPANY POLICY TO OFFER DISCOUNTS. WE TREAT ALL OUR CLIENTS EQUALLY AND FAIRLY.

FOR SPECIAL CLIENTS, I AM EMPOWERED TO GIVE 5% OFF IF YOU AGREE IMMEDIATELY. LET'S DO THE PAPER WORK NOW AND GO PLAY GOLF.

When the prospect asks for a discount . . .

you should delay giving the answer and provide other benefits of your product first. Otherwise the Hustler will immediately say the price *is* too high and ask for a discount. Not only will this reaction be quick, it will be sincere. You will find it difficult not to agree instinctively that your price is too high. If, on the other hand, you have provided and obtained enough agreed benefits, the Hustler's request for the discount will be slower and will sound more like a 'try-on' in tone.

As explained in the previous chapter Hustlers love to negotiate special discounts or bargains. If Hustlers are not given the opportunity to negotiate then they may well lack emotional commitment. A classic response adopted by many sales executives when confronted with Hustlers is to use the artificial discount discussed earlier. Another technique is to offer some other special feature, such as free installation, that has a high perceived value to the customer but a low cost to the selling company.

A good example of the artificial discount which I used in my selling career occurred when a computer company I was working for had a special incentive to remove refurbished tape drives from current stock. The book value of the units was $1,000 and the company offered as a bonus 50 per cent of any consideration obtained above book value. One client of mine who needed some tapes was a Hustler. He took up an offer to play a game of squash for $1,000 a point. For every point that he beat me by in a game we would deduct $1,000 from a proposed $20,000 selling price for the tapes. Five games later we signed a contract for $5,000 in the changing room. The client was happy — he thought he had just saved his company $15,000. I was happy — I had just earned $2,000 for losing a game of squash.

The other person who asks for a discount is the Normal. Not all Normals ask for a discount but those with purchasing experience do. The Normals have learned over time that if they ask for a discount they will get it from some salespeople. So asking for a discount has become a habit. Never give Normals a discount, however, because surprisingly, they do not want it! Normals have a strong sense of ethics. If you offer them a discount too easily, they will wonder what the last customer obtained and whether the price book changes for each client. If you refuse to provide a discount and accompany the refusal with a short explanation of how your company treats all clients the same and none is offered a discount, the explanation will be accepted with relief. You will, in fact, improve your credibility because the Normal will perceive you and your company as sound and ethical.

Loyalty to an Existing Supplier

This objection comes most often from Ditherers and Artists. Hustlers have little loyalty; they will usually switch suppliers at the drop of a price. Ditherers worry that if they change suppliers it will be a mistake. Artists also are oversensitive to the complaints that may come from current suppliers. Thus, the method of handling this objection depends on the component type.

Handle Ditherers by playing on the wish for change combined with the fear of taking risks. The ever-complaining Ditherer will have real and imagined incidents of dissatisfaction with the present suppliers. You should weaken their resolve by asking Ditherers why they should be loyal to just one supplier and so allow the supplier to charge monopoly prices. You should question whether their organisation expects them to be permanently loyal to its present suppliers and whether the company has ever changed suppliers in the past. If you are able to suggest a trial run with a money-back guarantee, you should be able to make the change appear free of risk.

Artists need a different approach. The secret is to ask them whether their own organisation is a joint supplier with a competitor to any of its clients. Then you should ask the Artist to imagine the difference in service and price that the customer with one supplier obtains, compared with the client who has two competing suppliers.

Moreover, you should ask the Artist to imagine how keen your company and the existing supplier would be about providing service if they were joint suppliers. If the joint supplier proposal is impossible then you will have to establish a relationship gradually over several short meetings. As Artists can prove to be stubbornly loyal, it may be a more profitable use of your own time to move on to another prospect.

I Will Not Make a Decision Now

You should remember that this objection is most commonly given by people who do not have the authority to make a decision. However, if you are talking to the decision maker and you do get this objection, the personality type is often the reason. Many sales textbooks suggest that, with this common objection, you ride roughshod over the prospect but the results of doing that can be disastrous. An understanding of personality types helps the salesperson to handle this objection.

The Engineer is probably working on one project and does not want to delay its progress by thinking about something else. Better tactics are to ask him or her about the present project and the timetable for its completion. Then aim at making the introduction of your product the next project and fix an appointment when you can next meet. Afterwards send the Engineer the thickest technical textbook you have on your product. What you must not do is interrupt the current timetable and so irritate the client.

Ask Hustlers why they will not make a decision and, after hearing a number of different stories, you will probably discover most just want a bigger discount.

Ask the Ditherer why and you will probably uncover another objection. However, you should realise that the Ditherer needs time to ponder decisions. He or she will want to double-check the decision with various people.

The Artist will want to reflect on the decision for a few days. Instead of being insensitive, suggest that you meet again to give the Artist time to think about it. Suggest that the agenda for the next meeting will be a further discussion which may lead to a decision. In the intervening period you should send the Artist a letter documenting all the agreed benefits, using visual words.

With the Normal, Mover and Politician a decision is often obtainable, so with them you should not give up. The easiest way is to ask the prospect why it is impossible to make a decision. Another good technique is just to say, 'Yes, I understand', pause for a few seconds and then continue with another benefit.

I Do Not Like Your Company

Companies have images and if the image of your company conflicts with the personality type of the prospect then you, as a salesperson, could have a major problem. The easiest way to handle this objection is to disarm it by bringing it out into the open. Then have a discussion with the prospect in which you differentiate between either the public image and the private reality or the old image and the new reality. Some examples of these basic objections and how to handle them are given below:

- *The Normal thinks your company is unethical.*
  Reference sell with overtly ethical clients such as doctors or banks.

- *The Hustler thinks your company lacks shrewdness.*
  Provide examples of situations in which your company has demonstrated cunning behaviour.

- *The Mover thinks your company is unfriendly.*
  Bring in some friendly colleagues and do some entertaining.

- *The Ditherer thinks your company is risky.*
  Dispel these doubts with your oldest and best references.

- *The Artist thinks your company is insensitive.*
  Agree with him or her, but then get the Artist to imagine how the managing director of your company could improve its sensitivity.

- *The Politician thinks your company is too small.*
  Ask him or her to provide an opinion on how to handle this objection.

- *The Engineer thinks your company is technically weak.*
  Ask for details of the objection, preferably written in a letter, and then reply with a comprehensive written answer and a demonstration.

If you fail to convince the prospect, you should not be afraid to give up and move on to another one. Selling is often regarded as a numbers game. Many companies have increased the productivity of their sales forces by teaching them about prospect qualification. They train the sales representative to first establish whether the prospect is a buyer by using something like the MAN mnemonic referred to in chapter 11 (does the prospect have the Money, the Authority to buy and the Need?), rather than starting with the product presentation. Using prospect qualification techniques means the sales force spends precious sales time on new prospects rather than wasting it on prospects who were never going to buy. Salespeople should follow the same tactic when faced with the objection that 'I do not like your company'.

I Do Not Like You

This objection is rarely covered in sales textbooks but experience and research suggest that antipathy to a salesperson is a far more common objection than is usually realised. Similar personality types tend to favour each other. As there are seven types and each person has one or two dominant components then the chances of these components matching during a sales interview are small. This is another reason why selling is sometimes regarded as a numbers game. If you talk to enough prospects you are bound to come across enough people similar to you in personality so you can act naturally and still close the sale.

To improve the closing ratio the salesperson should first establish the prospect's components, as outlined earlier. Then, like a chameleon, adapt your personality and adopt some of the mannerisms of the type you are addressing. For example, with a Mover smile, speak enthusiastically and look into the prospect's eyes. With an Artist, avoid eye contact, speak quietly and use visual words. For the Hustler, talk about money or recent gambling victories and offer to take the Hustler to lunch. Stress security with a Ditherer and put compassion and sincerity into your voice.

If you can have a second meeting, carefully analyse the prospect after the first meeting, establish the components and read the appropriate chapters to obtain an understanding of the prospect's personality. For the next meeting set yourself three goals on how you will tailor your behaviour to develop empathy and so be seen in a more favourable light.

What happens is that as you mimic the behaviour of the prospect, you develop an understanding of his or her personality. Consequently you should build a rapport with the prospect. It is in enabling salespeople to counter this most common objection, 'I do not like you', that Empathy Selling establishes itself as a powerful selling technique.

Bad Past Experience with Your Company

With luck this objection will not come up too often. The Politician is the person who usually harbours a grudge the longest. Handling this objection is easy; the secret is to change the objection from one of company to one of person and human error. All companies make some mistakes. If you can place the blame on a former employee or one who has moved to another state or department so much the better. If you gently suggest that the person at fault has been demoted or forced to leave while the Politician has remained and grown in status and prestige, you should defuse the objection. With other types, you should try to use statements like 'Water under the bridge', 'Nothing stands still' or 'You will be pleased to know our company has changed management, direction, policy, etc.'

Your Proposition Is Not Good Enough

The objection that your proposition is not good enough is rarely stated in such a fashion. The objection generally comes in two formats; either: 'Do you have it in pink?' or 'What if I need it in pink?'. Again a knowledge of personality types helps you to handle this objection.

Normals, Artists and Engineers will give your product a technical grilling and be looking for logical flaws in your presentation. It is with these three types that your product knowledge must be accurate. If you do not know the answer to a technical question say you do not know but will find out. You will not lose esteem but will gain respect and improve your credibility, provided you do follow up with the answer.

Hustlers and Politicians, on the other hand, will expect an immediate answer so, if necessary, improvise. You should not worry if you have to exaggerate or generalise because if they were in your shoes they would do the same. Use humour or a story to defuse the objection. Hustlers and Politicians never admit they were wrong or ignorant; it is important if you wish to remain credible with these two personality types that you do not either.

All five types (Normals, Artists, Engineers, Hustlers, and Politicians) will ask, 'Does the product come in pink?'.

The best way to answer this type of question was described by Tom Hopkins in his book *How to Master the Art of Selling*. The technique, known as the 'porcupine', is to answer the question with another question which suggests that the prospect will buy the product if the answer is favourable. For example, to the question 'Can we get this product in pink?' you should not just answer, 'Yes'. You should say 'Would you like it in pink?' This immediately puts the onus on the prospect to tell you whether the question is a real objection and whether the prospect intends to buy. Furthermore, if the product is available in pink, the prospect has said he wants it and not the salesperson. Prospects usually prefer to believe themselves rather than the salesperson and successful sales are often generated by prospects convincing themselves.

The Ditherer will ask a whole series of 'What if?' questions and by the end of a presentation, you will often wonder how you ever managed to sell anyone your product before. The technique for handling 'What if?' questions was described by Frank Bettger in *How I Rose from Failure to Success in Selling*. The secret is to 'ask why' and answer each question in turn, and then ask, 'Besides that, is there something else?'. Gradually, the Ditherer will realise that most of the objections are imaginary and start to present the real ones. Sometimes a salesperson begins to take the Ditherer's objections personally because there are so many of them. Try to remember that Ditherers complain to everyone and never take their many objections personally.

Conclusion

J. Pierpoint Morgan Senior, one of America's most famous bankers, once said: 'A man has two reasons for doing a thing — one that sounds good and a real one.' There are seven basic objections and an understanding of personality types will help the salesperson significantly in understanding the real objections and how to handle them.

Artists and Movers often fail to provide objections. Artists may have objections but be too shy to broach them. The best technique in this case is to draw the objections out tactfully and discuss them sensitively.

Movers are a much more difficult problem. They give you such a warm reception and greet your product so enthusiastically that you leave the meeting convinced you will get the order. Unfortunately, when you have gone the Mover forgets you. With the Mover you must be continuously closing — and closing is the subject of the next chapter.

CHAPTER 14

*C*LOSING TECHNIQUES

KEITH Stevenson, in his book *Go Selling*, defined closing as follows: 'Closing is what distinguishes the salesperson from the representative. The representative leaves the customer better informed and the salesperson leaves the customer with an order.' No better definition exists.

The subordinate question close works best with a P.

There are many closing techniques but, again, we will use a simple mnemonic that describes seven tried and proven methods. The mnemonic is ASPINIA. The ASPINIA is the brightest flower in the selling garden and is one that every salesperson should have, if not in a buttonhole, then inside his or her head. ASPINIA stands for the following seven closing techniques:

- Assume the Sale:
  'So how much trade-in were you hoping for on your current car?'
- Subordinate Question:
  'Are you going to buy a manual or automatic?'
- Physical action:
  'Let's go for a test drive.'
- Inducement:
  'We have been authorised to offer a 10 per cent discount to those clients who purchase by the end of the week.'
- Narrative Close:
  'We have agreed you want a blue automatic station wagon with power steering. Our other office can bring one over now. While that is being done, let's complete the documentation.'
- Impending Event:
  'The manufacturer has announced it will no longer be making this model so if you want it you should decide now.'
- Ask for the Order:
  'Shall we start drawing up the documentation now?'

Other closes could be added to this list but, as I explained before, you should never have more than seven items in a list. Seven closing techniques are enough for most salespeople.

Most selling textbooks begin the chapter on closing methods by first noting that many salespeople fail to get the order because they do not ask for it. Once that lesson has been learnt and the salesperson still fails to get the order the novice is told to try at least five closes during a presentation. While trying five closes generally improves the close/presentation ratio, the salesperson can become a particularly boring individual in the process, especially if the same closing technique is used again and again!

The closing rate improves when the salesperson tries a different close at each opportunity. Each of the seven closes listed above appeals most to a certain personality type. If the salesperson tries the closing technique which matches the personality type the probability of a successful close rises substantially.

Salespeople who use Empathy Selling already know which closing technique appeals to which component type so, after they have determined the dominant components of the personality of the prospect, they use those closing techniques that are more likely to lead to success.

Assume the Sale

The first technique, Assume the Sale, works best with Ditherers, who often like others to make decisions for them.

I remember a department store refrigerator saleswoman who provided a good example of the Assume-the-Sale close. After the prospect entered the store the professional would immediately usher the family past all the refrigerators to her desk where they would all sit down. She would then pick out an order form and fill it in while she asked the prospect various questions such as name, address, size of family (which dictated refrigerator size), special likes and dislikes, and so on. When the form was completed she would repeat all the details and then mark a large and heavy X next to each place where the prospect was to sign. She would then say: 'Is that right, Ms Blank?' and place the form in front of the prospect. She would then shut up and not say a word because she knew the next person to speak loses. There would usually be a long silence, often lasting up to five minutes. The customer would then smile, shrug and sign.

When I first heard this technique described, I refused to believe it. Nobody would do that, I thought. Two days later my managing director gave me fifty raffle tickets to sell for a local hospital board of which my managing director was a member. As he gave me the tickets he told me that none were to be returned. I was going to a party that night and I decided I would test the Assume-the-Sale technique.

At the party I went up to complete strangers, smiled and introduced myself. I then asked them for their name and address and filled in the details on the ticket. I then said the ticket cost a dollar, handed it over and asked if the name and address were correct. Then I would say nothing. I gave no details of the prizes or the raffle. Only one person refused to hand over a dollar. Fifty people out of fifty-one gave me a dollar in silence with no questions asked! I became an instant convert to the Assume-the-Sale technique.

The technique is particularly powerful with the most difficult type to close — the Ditherer. It works with the Ditherer because it provides little opportunity to procrastinate over a decision — it allows no freedom of choice. Ditherers will usually make a decision when there is only one choice; if offered a diversity of solutions they will not choose. Ditherers have not realised the turtle only makes progress when it sticks its neck out.

Subordinate Question Technique

The Subordinate Question technique changes the buying decision from a major one (should I buy this product or not?) to a minor one (should it be in red or blue?). It is sometimes referred to as 'closing on a minor point'.

This is the closing technique most appropriate for the Politician. Politicians delight in making decisions so the more you can give them the happier they will be. Make the close a whole series of subordinate questions such as:

'Do you want a black one or brown one?'
'Do you want power steering or power brakes?'

By contrast, this method is a complete failure with a Ditherer. Ask a Ditherer a series of subordinate questions and you will most likely delay the sale by months.

Physical Action or 'Puppy Dog'

The Physical-Action close is sometimes defined as handing the prospect a pen, opening the cash register and preparing an order form. These are, in fact, examples of the Assume-the-Sale close. The Physical-Action close entails the prospect becoming involved in some physical action with the product. A good example of this technique is the variation known as the Puppy-Dog Close when, for example, you put a water cooler into an office for a two-week free trial. By the end of the trial, the staff are so enamoured of the product that they refuse to part with it. It is just like putting a strange puppy dog into a home. Soon it becomes a pet.

The Physical-Action close works best with Engineers. They like to get involved with any new product by trying it out and seeing if it works. If you time the introduction of a free trial so the Engineer has sufficient opportunity to evaluate the product then you will usually get the order if the product itself is satisfactory.

The Physical-Action technique, while excellent for an Engineer, can be a disaster with a Hustler. The Hustler is by nature too lazy to try the product and will try to persuade someone else to do the physical evaluation. However, if you try to take the product away, the Hustler will plead for another month. After six months the Hustler will then return it saying that your major competitor has also offered a free trial. The Hustler will tell you that while your product is preferred, it is company policy to be fair and give competitors a reasonable opportunity. After twelve months neither you nor your competitor will finish with an order but the Hustler would have had one year's free use of your company's and your competitor's products.

Inducement

This technique covers all the various inducements such as two years' warranty instead of one, 10 per cent discount if you sign now and so on. The Inducement sale is the ideal technique for the Hustler. Try to offer an inducement that costs your company a limited amount but is perceived as good value by the prospect.

Inducement sales do not appeal to the Normal as they imply a potential reduction in quality and make the Normal suspicious of either the product, the supplier or you.

Narrative Close

The Narrative Close is the one in which the salesperson reiterates the benefits and, if possible, uses some third party as a referral. The Narrative technique works best with people with a lot of

Normal component. Because of their dominant desire for social approval Normals prefer products which have the endorsement of other users. They also prefer logic (seen as mature) to emotion (seen as childish) and find the logical nature of the Narrative close especially appealing. Among adults the Normal is probably the most common dominant component and this explains why the Narrative close is one of the most successful.

A derivation of the Narrative technique is the 'Benjamin Franklin close', named after its famous inventor, the American statesman. In this close the salesperson draws a line down the centre of a piece of paper and titles the two columns Yes and No. Under the Yes column the salesperson slowly lists every agreed benefit. Under the No column the customer is asked to list every point against the product. Both columns are tallied and the logical decision is made. After the Assume-the-Sale technique the Benjamin Franklin close is probably the easiest technique to use, but even experienced salespeople seldom use it. Novice sales executives would do well to practise it because, of all sales techniques, it makes most use of the axiom that seven out of eight people prefer to think they buy rather than that they are sold.

Impending Event

The Impending Event, such as price rises, material shortages or industrial disputes is a well-known and often-tried technique which usually fails because most people are optimistic and do not believe that a disaster will strike soon. It is often used as a fear close on Ditherers, with mixed results. The Impending Event close works best with someone who can imagine the effects of an Impending Event and the personality type with the best imagination is the Artist. The Impending Event close is therefore most successful with the Artist.

Ask for the Order

Asking for the order in a blunt, forthright manner works best with the Mover. Movers tend to be insensitive so using an insensitive method is particularly apt. The Mover will need to be closed repeatedly — just ask for the order in a casual, confident and friendly manner again, and again and again. Movers need to be liked and abhor rejection. Once they begin to believe that they will jeopardise the friendly (albeit temporary) relationship with you if they do not sign, you will then probably close the sale.

Conclusion

Closing is what distinguishes the salesperson from the representative. A representative never tries to close because he or she fears rejection; in fact, representatives are sometimes called 'colourful closers' because they are thought to be yellow.

The salesperson who will succeed most is the one who realises that the personality type of the prospect must determine closing technique. There are many other closing methods and every salesperson has favourites, but no single method works every time with all individuals. You should now try to identify which of your favourite closing techniques would work best with each of the seven personality types. Then, in closing situations, apply the appropriate closing technique after you have analysed the prospect. If you do this systematically rather than haphazardly, your close rate should improve. The table below summarises the best closing method for each component type.

Type	Closing Technique
Normal	Narrative
Hustler	Inducement
Mover	Ask for the Order
Ditherer	Assume the Sale
Artist	Impending Event
Politician	Subordinate Question
Engineer	Puppy Dog

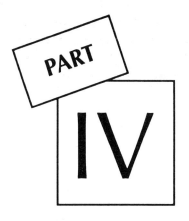

FINE-TUNING YOUR TECHNIQUE

*P*ERSONALITY COMBINATIONS

S O far we have only considered stereotypes which are personalities obsessively dominated by a single component. In the chapter about the Normal, however, we discussed combinations of the Normal with another component to show how the Normal was an integrating and moderating influence. Most personalities you will meet will be average to high Normal combined with two other dominant components which may reinforce or conflict with other. It is this reinforcement or tension that accounts for much of the diversity of human nature and is the basis of the Somerset Maugham quote at the begining of this book. We all have some of each component within us and each component has some influence on our behaviour.

Excluding the Normal there are fifteen double combinations of personality components, as the table on page 111 shows. The most common type of combination is the E-I, in which an extrovert component (Mover, Ditherer or Hustler) combines with an introvert component (Artist, Politician or Engineer). In these combinations there is a natural psychological tension. As the table demonstrates, there are nine E-I combinations. The other two types of combination are either extrovert with extrovert (E-E) or introvert with introvert (I-I). There are three of each of these and they lead to the Jungian stereotypes discussed in Chapter 18.

Each of the double combinations will be covered in turn. The double combination can be described in one of two ways, either as an Artist-Hustler or a Hustler-Artist. The choice merely depends on convention or which abbreviation sounds the more pleasant.

Dual Component Combinations

	M	D	H	A	P	E
M		E-E	E-E	E-I	E-I	E-I
D			E-E	E-I	E-I	E-I
H				E-I	E-I	E-I
A					I-I	I-I
P						I-I

Mover-Hustler (M-H)

Mover-Hustlers crave excitement and have a short-term view of life. They tend to be friendly yet superficial. If they also have a strong Normal component they will use their self-control to turn their energetic cunning into an aggressive and successful business. When you sell to Mover-Hustlers, appeal to their active short-term desire for material success.

Mover-Ditherer (M-D)

This combination has already been covered in the chapter on the Ditherer component. Mover-Ditherers oscillate between enthusiasm for your product and lethargy and inattention. If the sale needs repeated meetings their mercurial mood changes can prove to be exhausting. The best selling approach is to stress the social benefits of your product or service first. You should also try to spread any perceived buying risk among as many people in the Mover-Ditherer's organisation as possible.

Mover-Artist (M-A)

The Mover-Artist is another combination full of tension. The sociability of the Mover strains against the shyness of the Artist. This can lead to paradoxical behaviour with the buyer one moment waxing enthusiastic and the next moment being passively stubborn. Mover-Artists must be handled carefully as they may get carried away about your product and attribute to it features it does not have. This overenthusiasm may thus lead to unfortunate repercussions after the sale.

Mover-Politician (M-P)

Mover-Politicians are energetic, talkative and argumentative. Provided they have a reasonable degree of self-control, they will strive for and often achieve leadership positions. They are often decision-makers. If you show Mover-Politicians that the product has social benefits and will provide them with credit and recognition then they will usually buy.

Good techniques are to structure the sale into a series of subordinate closes and to use reference sells to support your argument such as 'Many partners of the large professional accountant firms would consider . . .'

Mover-Politicians are also impressed with meeting important people so it is a good strategy to introduce them to important people in your organisation or those employed by your reference sales.

Mover-Engineer (M-E)

Mover-Engineers also suffer psychological stress because the desire of the Engineer to concentrate on and complete one project conflicts with the desire of the Mover to move on and meet somebody different. Once they have decided on a project, Mover-Engineers try single-mindedly to finish it, with impatient forcefulness. Once they are convinced that your product has a useful goal and social benefits, they will usually become talkative and fervent supporters of it.

When selling to Mover-Engineers you need to make sure that they do not get carried away with some method of using your product that subsequently turns out to be impractical and so cause the sale to be lost. Mover-Engineers are prone to go off on wild goose chases.

They may also have emotional outbursts that end in sheepish apologies. If this happens pay no attention to them, just excuse yourself and say that you will return in a few minutes.

Ditherer-Hustler (D-H)

Ditherer-Hustlers are often suspicious that there is something wrong with your product and that the price is too high. In the same way ferrets hunt out choice rabbits from their burrows, Ditherer-Hustlers try to find the best deal possible. They take a long time to reach a decision and are always nibbling away for something better. Instead of overreacting to their questions and spending too much time with them it is better to answer questions directly and then leave them alone for a few moments to digest the answer.

If you do have a product or service that provides value for money Ditherer-Hustlers will eventually buy. They become useful after the purchase because they are famous among their contemporaries for being careful, fastidious bargain hunters, and are therefore the best references of all to have.

Ditherer-Artist (D-A)

Ditherer-Artists are sheltered, timid personalities; for example, they are often hypochondriacs. They must be among the hardest people to sell to, because they can imagine all sorts of deficiencies and problems to do with introducing your product or service. When salespeople encounter a Ditherer-Artist in a decision-making role they should carefully evaluate whether it might prove more profitable to move onto another prospect — a sale to a Ditherer-Artist is usually protracted. A good compromise is to try to kill two birds with one stone. Keep the meetings short and arrange to have a meeting with another prospect nearby.

A good technique for selling to a Ditherer-Artist is just to stare at him or her in a friendly fashion, saying nothing and lifting your eyebrows expectantly. The silence produces anxiety, causing the Ditherer-Artist to talk first. He or she may even end up buying your product to prevent further embarrassment.

When selling to a D-A just stare at him or her in a friendly fashion, saying nothing and lifting your eyebrows expectantly.

Ditherer-Politician (D-P)

A Ditherer-Politician whose Normal component is low can be a most unpleasant combination. People with it tend to have a veneer of confidence but underneath feel insecure and inferior. The desire to win does not sit comfortably with the desire for security.

Ditherer-Politicians will spend time criticising anything new about your product and pointing out sarcastically all the ways it can go wrong.

They are the warthogs of human society (warthogs are the ugliest of all the African animals). It is easy to sell to them; just remember that beneath the rough exterior of a Ditherer-Politician there is an obnoxious bore.

Never agree or disagree with the Ditherer-Politician's comments. It is best simply to press on, disregarding any criticisms and suggesting that concrete answers are better than abstract problems. If you keep up the single minded pressure the Ditherer-Politician should soon become a client. Your reward will not just be the sale itself; the Ditherer-Politician will become one of your company's best references.

Ditherer-Engineer (D-E)

Ditherer-Engineers are also difficult buyers. Not only will they find fault with your product, they will do so in excruciating detail. The secret is to let them complain about their present methods as much as possible. If you appeal to their need for change and demonstrate how simple your product will be to introduce, Ditherer-Engineers, after many protracted meetings, may decide that your product is a promising solution.

To convince a Ditherer-Engineer you should provide considerable documentation about the technical qualities of your product and a list of happy customers. If you are selling a new product or service you may make better use of your valuable selling time by finding new prospects and returning to the Ditherer-Engineer when you have a number of satisfied clients to refer to.

Artist-Hustler (A-H)

The Artist-Hustler is another tense combination. The Hustler's desire for material success combined with the Artist's creative desire means that people with this personality combination can devise quite cunning schemes for making money. If they have a weak Normal component, Artist-Hustlers may have a veneer of sincerity but underneath they will be cynical in handling people and may take part in subterfuge. They are quick to change the topic when you are selling to them and will not respond to a direct attack. When selling to them remember that they are sometimes sneaky. If you can come up with an imaginative, shrewd use of your product and also appeal to the 'What's in it for me?' factor, you will perhaps obtain business from them.

Artist-Politician (A-P)

The Artist-Politician is the traditional split personality. He or she can be withdrawn in one meeting and aggressive during the next. It is difficult to develop empathy with Artist-Politicians as they are difficult to approach and frequently appear cold and unresponsive. Although Artist-Politicians are often out of touch with reality, they hold their unrealistic views with fierce obstinacy.

Artist-Engineer (A-E)

This is the most introverted combination. A typical Artist-Engineer is an inventor or research scientist working alone on some imaginative, inspired project. The Artist-Engineer does not relate to people and appears bashful and shy.

When selling to Artist-Engineers restrain your enthusiasm and get them to express their own ideas. Ask them to imagine practical uses of your product. If they show any signs of withdrawal or irritability you should defer discussion and arrange a subsequent meeting. One good technique is to appeal to the prospect's sense of what is best for the company.

Politician-Engineer (P-E)

Politician-Engineers are the pedantic project managers. They will seek perfection from a product just as they do from themselves or their subordinates. They believe they are never wrong and actively seek recognition of their achievements.

If you can demonstrate some inspired use of your product and show how the introduction of the product will improve the status of the Politician-Engineer among his or her peers or in the organisation, you will improve your chances of getting the sale.

To succeed with a Politician-Engineer you must know your product intimately. Instead of arguing over technical points use extension questions such as 'How will this work with other parts of your organisation?' to develop the Politician-Engineer's enthusiasm for your product or service. In time, he or she may consider that introducing your company's product will be a worthy project and one which may bring substantial kudos to the buyer.

Hustler-Politician (H-P)

The Hustler's desire for material success combined with the Politician's desire to win can make the Hustler-Politician an unpleasant personality. Hustler-Politicians tend to be excessively suspicious and they can behave like camels — snooty, arrogant and autocratic. If you believe that they are sniping at your product, stop them by asking them to explain or expand their comments. They are susceptible to flattery as they combine the large egos of both the Politician and Hustler. If their Normal component is low they can be greedy, too, and under stress they may be jealous and touchy, so they must be treated with kid gloves. One selling tactic is to stress indirectly how your product or service will provide immediate gain and recognition once the Hustler-Politician has committed his or her organisation.

Hustler-Engineer (H-E)

The Hustler-Engineer is another interesting combination. The desire for material success often leads the Hustler to take a short-term perspective, while the Engineer takes a long-term view of life. This leads to psychological tension.

Hustler-Engineers tend to prefer flashy products with many gadgets and technical points. They often have complicated stereo equipment or sports cars.

Hustler-Engineers also tend to be erratic about making decisions because they are always wondering whether something better might come along. You should sell your product as a new solution and appeal to their imaginations before they change their minds.

Summary

Combinations add to the diversity of the personality. I have tried to show in this chapter that if you are familiar with the basic seven components then developing a selling strategy for the double combination is not difficult. You can use the same process when you get three strong components or strong and weak components mixed together.

However, as a salesperson, you should now be able to understand why the personalities of different buyers and clients can be so diverse. You now understand how important it is to develop empathy. You should also realise that to succeed, you need to tailor your sales approach to the personality of the buyer.

A CHAPTER 16
ANALYSING YOURSELF

MANY textbooks have said that a key to selling success is to gain empathy with the prospect. The key message of this book is to show that salespeople can succeed in gaining empathy with clients by altering their personalities to fit that of their clients. To succeed in this technique you must know your own personality, which is the subject of this chapter.

By now you should have some idea of your own dominant components, keeping in mind that each component exists to some degree in every individual. The diversity of personalities among the human race is accounted for by the mixture of the relative strengths of each. For example, if there were just three levels of strength for the seven components then it would be possible to describe 2,187 different personalities.

Profile of the Ideal Salesperson

One reason salespeople should know their own personality is that they need to know how suited they are to the selling profession. One technique is to compare yourself to the ideal profile. The following is a profile of the ideal sales executive which I have generated over time.

Normal

The desire for social approval should not be too high. Successful salespeople often have to break the 'rules' to get the order. Therefore the Normal component should be average to weak, because selling is an emotional process and a high Normal will usually rely too much on logic.

Mover

The desire to communicate with people and the energy level should be high. Good salespeople generally like meeting people.

Ditherer

The desire for security should be low, because the salesperson must be prepared to take risks. Too strong a desire for security is incompatible with sales, and good salespeople enjoy living by their wits.

Artist

If the desire to be creative is too strong then the salesperson may spend too much time thinking about clever uses or expensive custom product designs rather than thinking about the customer's needs. The Artist component should be average to low because, although the Artist's imagination and sensitivity would be useful in establishing empathy, selling is a social process and Artists are usually shy.

Politician

Good selling is a win-win situation and the desire to win must be strong in a good sales representative. Most selling situations also involve at least one competitor. The Politician component should be high as good salespeople need the desire to beat the competition and win.

Engineer

A good salesperson should not have too high an Engineer component or he or she will be more interested in describing the technical details of the product than selling it. When I was a computer salesman one of my mentors told me never to confuse selling with implementation. What he meant was that the customer bought what he *wanted*. Later, during the implementation of the system, the customer discovered what he *needed* and then

Too much E in a sales executive can mean too much emphasis on the product and not enough on developing empathy with the prospect.

the project managers and service system staff had to carry out a secondary selling activity. Sales executives with too much Engineer component tend to become overinvolved in the detail and often mar an otherwise successful implementation by not letting go.

Hustler

The desire for material success should be average to strong in a salesperson. Most organisations reward their sales staff with some form of bonus or commission and with a weak Hustler component an individual will not be motivated. A high Hustler component also ensures that the salesperson is shrewd, a necessary quality.

Very few people have every aspect of this profile and so there are few natural salespeople. Most salespeople fit the ideal selling profile only partially, and it is helpful to know which components you are lacking in and what you can do to adjust your behaviour in order to be a better salesperson.

Horses for Courses

There is another reason you should know your own personality. Although you may have some of the right components to be a successful salesperson, you may be in the wrong type of selling. The structure above describes the perfect salesperson but it is not often realised that there are different types of selling and that certain components will help you more in some types of selling than others.

A job description for a salesperson may be summed up by the mnemonic APC which stands for Appointment, Presentation and Close. Although this basic principle of selling should never be forgotten, it does fail to distinguish among the various images conjured up by the phrases 'door-to-door', 'account executive', 'marketing consultant', 'overseas banking representative' and so forth. All these individuals sell in some way but each type of selling requires different personality components for success.

It is possible to generalise the various types of selling by industry; such as retail, wholesale, office equipment, finance, etc. However, it is more useful to differentiate according to the type of presentation required.

Presentation Types

Experience has shown that there are three types of presentation: the Canned, the Outlined and the Programmed.

- *The Canned Presentation* resembles an advertisement. It consists of a formal script in which the benefits of the product are described in a logical sequence and the salesperson finishes by asking for the order.

- *The Outlined Presentation* occurs when a salesperson is selling a product with a wide range of benefits. Typically, the salesperson must discover the needs of the prospect by probing, satisfy those needs with the necessary benefits, overcome objections and then close. The salesperson usually uses some form of sales demonstration aid such as a brochure or model of the product.

- *The Programmed Presentation* is used with large accounts. In this presentation, it is necessary first to establish the decision-making structure. Secondly, the salesperson must meet the decision maker and establish the organisation's needs and the decision maker's wants. If the product appears to meet these requirements, then the salesperson generally has to carry out a survey with the people who are going to use the product and also some technical experts. Assuming the product does meet the technical and end-user requirements, the salesperson then returns to the decision maker with the results of the survey, makes a major presentation and then closes. The sale may take many visits and may last over a protracted period — on some large defence and computer contracts, for example, a sale may last more than five years! Yet, during all that time, the sale follows a definite programme.

The table below describes each presentation type distinguished by some variables.

The Types of Presentation

	Type of Sale		
Variable	Canned	Outlined	Programmed
Number of decision makers	one	usually two	several
Technical complexity of product	low	medium	high
Purchase risk	low	medium	high
Close rate	daily	weekly	monthly
Product expertise required by salesperson	low	medium	high
Typical product	cosmetics	car	aircraft

Each of these three presentation methods requires different sales techniques and personality types:

- The Canned Presentation requires the salesperson to be skilled in time and territory management, instant empathy and presentation design. The salesperson also needs the vigour to make many calls. If a salesperson who is required to do many Canned Presentations lacks a strong Mover component, the result will probably be failure.

- The Outlined Presentation requires the salesperson to be skilful in probing, objection handling and closing. The salesperson should be shrewd and good at establishing whether the prospect is a china egg (a prospect that will never break). Traditionally this area pays salespeople with high commission structures. If the salesperson lacks the desire for material success then this type of selling is usually difficult. Hustlers prefer Outlined Presentation selling.

- The Programmed Presentation is traditionally a long sale and competition is almost always present. The salesperson must be able to write an original proposal tailored to the prospect. The proposal should detail how the product or service solves the problems faced by the prospect. To be successful in this type of selling the salesperson needs to have a strong desire to win. Without a strong Politician component, this type of selling is difficult.

Client Empathy

The final reason you need to know your own personality is so you can moderate your behaviour to gain empathy and support from your prospects and clients. Changing your behaviour can become an important part of your sales strategy. For example, if your personality has a strong Mover component this will be helpful in overcoming the pessimism of the Ditherer. On the other hand the Mover's sociability should be subjugated when faced with the shyness of the Artist. Many lost sales can be traced to personality conflicts.

A knowledge of your own personality and how to adapt it can thus help you increase your sales success. How then do you find out your personality type? One way is to go to a trained psychologist and fill out a personality questionnaire such as the Humm-Wadsworth Test, for which Chandler & Macleod Consultants hold the copyright. It is possible to do the actual test by going to the original paper (see References page 136) but to calculate the results does require some professional skill. Another way is to buy the Pelican paperback, *Know Your Own Personality*, by H. Eysenck and G. Wilson, which has a number of tests which will allow you to develop a personality profile of yourself.

Alternatively you can use the quick checklist test provided in the next chapter. The purpose of the checklist is to provide a simple and quick way of analysing prospects. However, you could get someone, such as a spouse or close friend, to use it to analyse you.

A QUICK PERSONALITY CHECKLIST

ANSWER the questions quickly, spending no more than several seconds per line. The whole test should take no more than two minutes. Then complete the personality profile at the end of the test.

Normal	Yes	No
• On time and observes social graces	____	____
• Calls in experts and other people present	____	____
• Undue concern for precedent and approval	____	____
• Finishes with action plan	____	____
• Conservative clothing	____	____
• Reserved manner and unemotional	____	____
• Self-composed and calm	____	____
• Logical way of talking	____	____
• Tidy desk, office and dress	____	____
• Strong sense of morals and ethics	____	____
Yes scores out of 10	____	

Hustler	Yes	No
• Ostentatious jewellery, flashy watch	___	___
• Glitzy clothes (reds and oranges)	___	___
• Name dropper and cheaper designer labels	___	___
• First names and smiles	___	___
• Constant eye contact	___	___
• Appears to show genuine interest	___	___
• Egocentric	___	___
• Gambler or risk taker	___	___
• Obviously calculating best approach	___	___
• Talks money early and wants discount	___	___
Yes scores out of 10	___	

Mover	Yes	No
• Late for appointment but apologises	___	___
• First names	___	___
• Smiler, approachable, friendly	___	___
• Shows genuine interest	___	___
• Big picture, not detail	___	___
• Readily distracted by interruptions	___	___
• Socialises before coming to business	___	___
• Quick enthusiastic talker	___	___
• Speaks with hands	___	___
• Dress and make-up often untidy	___	___
Yes scores out of 10	___	

Ditherer	Yes	No
• Hypochondriac	___	___
• Conservative hair style	___	___
• Socialises before coming to business	___	___
• Earth colours in dress: browns and greens	___	___
• Picture of family in office	___	___
• Impacts as submissive	___	___
• Heavy smoker	___	___
• Stuffed handbag or office filled with files	___	___
• Minor problems seem insurmountable	___	___
• Picks undesirable features of proposal	___	___
Yes scores out of 10	___	

Artist	Yes	No
• No first names; no talk of family	___	___
• Avoids eye contact	___	___
• Shy and quiet	___	___
• Men have beards; women have long hair	___	___
• Sometimes stutters or stammers	___	___
• Hands over mouth pointing to eyes	___	___
• Non-egocentric	___	___
• Creative clothes and accessories	___	___
• Modern art in office	___	___
• Uses visual words	___	___
Yes scores out of 10	___	

Politician	Yes	No
• No first names	___	___
• Keeps you waiting and no apologies	___	___
• Quick on title, position and importance	___	___
• Constant self-referral, name dropping	___	___
• Displays status symbols in office	___	___
• Power dresser, blues and yellows	___	___
• Defends fixed opinions skilfully	___	___
• Uses auditory words	___	___
• Domineering, aggressive and truculent	___	___
Yes scores out of 10	___	

Engineer	Yes	No
• No first names and appears indifferent	___	___
• Pens in pocket or glasses on chain	___	___
• Details, not big picture	___	___
• Unemotional — yet suddenly enthusiastic	___	___
• Uses feeling words but monotonous tones	___	___
• Deliberate, single-minded	___	___
• Office full of books	___	___
• Untidy desk or big full handbag	___	___
• Likes a drink	___	___
• Project timetable on wall	___	___
Yes scores out of 10	___	

Simply count the number of yes answers for each component and draw a column graph. Seven or more 'yes' answers indicates a strong component which you could use to develop a selling strategy.

Sample Quick Check-List Graph

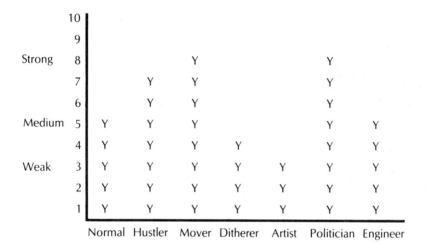

		Normal	Hustler	Mover	Ditherer	Artist	Politician	Engineer
	10							
	9							
Strong	8			Y			Y	
	7		Y	Y			Y	
	6		Y	Y			Y	
Medium	5	Y	Y	Y			Y	Y
	4	Y	Y	Y	Y		Y	Y
Weak	3	Y	Y	Y	Y	Y	Y	Y
	2	Y	Y	Y	Y	Y	Y	Y
	1	Y	Y	Y	Y	Y	Y	Y

The ideal salesperson of large computer systems would have a personality profile similar to the above graph.

CHAPTER 18

CONCLUSION

THE objective of this book is to describe a method that will help you close more sales more quickly and develop better client relationships. If you have read this far you should have gained an understanding of how personality analysis can help you develop empathy with prospects by adjusting your own behaviour and adapting different sales presentations. There is no more powerful weapon in marketing than satisfying the desires of buyers and Empathy Selling gives you a tool for direct selling.

This book does not aim at making you a trained psychologist and you will fail if you think personality analysis is your only selling tool. Empathy Selling does not replace product knowledge, telephone technique or selling strategies; it complements them.

Another trap when using Empathy Selling is to overanalyse the prospect. The secret is to establish only one or two dominant components and tailor your sales presentation according to them. A trap novice practitioners sometimes fall into is to spend too much time on analysis, because it is fun, and not enough on working out a successful sales plan.

Many people are as yet unaware of the sophistication of personality testing and the discrimination that researchers have managed to build into their tests. I remember a feature article in an English Sunday newspaper in the late 1960s. The article described an experiment in which a psychologist had each of seven famous people fill out a personality test questionnaire. From the test results the psychologist produced seven psychological profiles which in turn were all sent to the seven participants, who were asked to choose the one they thought best described their own personality.

DEGREES ON WALL—
HIGH 'P'

TINTED GLASSES —
MUST BE AN 'H'

PENS IN POCKET—
LOTS OF 'E'

FAMILY PICTURE
ON DESK —
MUST BE A 'D'

ROLLED UP SLEEVES —
HIGH 'M'

CONSULTANT'S REPORT
ON DESK —
MUST BE A 'D'

Beware of overanalysis!

The results of the experiment were illuminating — each of the seven participants correctly chose his own profile! The odds of this occurring are 1 in 823,543 or slightly more than picking the ace of spades three times in a row from a pack of shuffled cards. I remember when I read this article how surprised I was that personality testing had reached such a level of precision.

In 1973 I began my selling career, after completing a Master of Business Administration. I was following the advice of one of my lecturers who, at graduation time, had suggested that if I wanted to learn about business I should forget the MBA and go and sell. Like many new salespeople my enthusiasm soon had me devouring as many books and courses about selling as I could.

The books and courses were of two types. Ex-salespeople wrote the first type which were descriptions of tools and techniques they had collected over their careers. Professional educators, recognising that sales was probably the most important determinant of business success, wrote the second type, trying to create a structured training course. Both types of books and courses were helpful, but neither provided the key to selling — how to gain empathy with prospects and clients.

Personality theories to help us understand emotions have been proposed and recorded since the time of the ancient Greeks. However, it is only in the last fifty years that psychologists have developed techniques to analyse the personality scientifically. One such method consists of giving many people a series of questionnaires. The answers to the questionnaires may then be processed by a statistical technique developed in the 1930s known as 'multivariate analysis'. From this statistical analysis psychologists have established the presence of sixteen to twenty personality factors.

Psychologists, aided by computers, have refined personality questionnaires considerably. Psychological profiles are now produced which are completely descriptive of the person tested. So the results of the experiment described at the beginning of this chapter would have been no surprise to the knowledgeable.

While the ability to neatly measure the personality of a prospect is now possible it is unfortunately not practicable for a salesperson. To begin a sales interview with the suggestion that the prospect answer a one-hour questionnaire would be novel, but the likelihood of success is low! Some personal computer programs are now becoming available that allow the salesperson to analyse a prospect after the sales call and then suggest follow-up strategies. Unfortunately many sales calls are one-off, so the salesperson needs a tool that can be used during the first and what may be the only presentation.

Another problem is the number of different factors. To try to remember how to recognise sixteen to twenty personality traits and then how to adapt to them is beyond the capacity of most people. As discussed earlier a learning system is most useful if it requires you to learn no more than seven points.

That is why we have used an early theory of the personality, first stated in 1924 by the American psychologist Rosanoff. Until the work of Rosanoff, doctors defined abnormal psychological conditions in black and white — a person was either mad or not. Rosanoff suggested that such a distinction between the normal and abnormal states was artificial and the difference was not one of kind but of degree. Normality and abnormality should not be thought of as black and white but as different shades of grey. This view of mental illness as a point on a continuum has since become the modern view. Rosanoff further noted that there were few mental illnesses and proposed a theory of personality based on the most common four:

- schizophrenia;
- epilepsy;
- hysteria;
- cyclodia (what we now call manic depression).

Rosanoff included a fifth component called the Normal. This component may best be understood as the desire for social approval, associated with behaviour such as social adjustment or integration with society. It is best expressed as the gradual change that occurs to the personality as the human being matures — and then may fade away if the adult enters a second childhood.

Two southern Californian psychologists, Humm and Wadsworth, used multivariate analysis to extend the Rosanoff hypothesis by dividing cyclodia and schizophrenia into two components each. This resulted in seven personality temperament components.

As professional salespeople we are not so much interested in analysing people in depth as we are keen to try and establish their basic buying motivations. Associated with each of the seven components is a basic desire. While it would have been possible to use the original Rosanoff terms throughout this book, the terms are alien to most readers and are associated with mental illness. For sales staff it is better to eliminate jargon and use terms that convey the buying desire and correlate with our seven stereotypes, as in the table below.

The Dominant Desires and Stereotypes

Rosanoff Term	Stereotype	Dominant Desire
Normal	Normal	Desire for social approval
Manic	Mover	Desire to communicate
Depressive	Ditherer	Desire for security
Autistic	Artist	Desire to be creative
Paranoid	Politician	Desire to win
Epileptoid	Engineer	Desire to complete projects
Hysteroid	Hustler	Desire for material success

The reader should remember, when using Empathy Selling, that it is a simplification and accuracy is sacrificed.

On the other hand, the means of obtaining the necessary degree of accuracy when selling is generally unavailable — if you can get prospects to sit two-hour personality tests, perhaps you should think about selling personality tests as a career!

The personality stereotypes defined by Empathy Selling lack the precision of subsequent research, but that is not a reason to refuse to use Empathy Selling. A good analogy is a sailor's use of celestial navigation to establish a ship's location. Celestial navigation is based on the hypothesis that the earth is fixed and the stars and the sun revolve around the earth. Since the time of Copernicus we have known this hypothesis to be false, and it is possible to use the laws of relativity to calculate one's position accurately. However, the calculations are laborious and complex and, without a computer, impractical. By using a sextant and the hypothesis that the sun and the stars revolve around a fixed earth, sailors can quite easily fix their position with a sufficient degree of accuracy for their purposes.

It is also useful to relate some personality theories, both historical and modern, to Empathy Selling. Jung, for example, divided the world into extroverts and introverts. Extroverts are people whose fundamental interest is the outer or objective world. They tend to be gregarious and spontaneous. They prefer to participate in social affairs. Introverts, on the other hand, have a preference for the world of imagination and contemplation. They tend to be more sensitive and subject their thoughts to more analysis and criticism. They tend to submerge their emotions and prefer their own company to that of others.

Typically most adults can be described as average to high Normal component, one dominant extrovert and one dominant introvert component. If, however, the personality is influenced by two dominant introvert or two dominant extrovert components then the individual will tend towards either of the two stereotypes postulated by Jung.

Another theory which has recently become popular among salespeople is neuro-linguistic programming or NLP. This hypothesis, which was postulated by two research scientists, Richard Bandler and John Grinder, proposes that people receive data from the outside world mainly by the eye, the ear or touch. Furthermore they hypothesise that people tend to prefer one channel to the others and this preference can be recognised by a number of

clues, especially the language they use. The three channels are
described as the visual, auditory and kinaesthetic. These three
channels correspond to the Artist, Politician and Engineer
components. As most individuals have at least one dominant
introvert component, there is a correlation with neuro-linguistic
programming.

The scientific analysis of personality using questionnaires is a
relatively new science. It is only recently that biochemists have
begun to suggest theories for the causes of personality types. One
theory relates the degree of the Mover and Ditherer components
to the amounts of certain neuro-transmitters in the body. Neuro-
transmitters are small molecules that act as chemical communicators between neurons. There is another theory, developed from
CAT-scans of the brain, that suggests that the amount of Artist
and Politician components are related to the size of certain cav-
ities in the brain called the ventricles. Other studies postulate
hereditary factors as a reason for personality types.

What is certain is that personality analysis in selling will
become increasingly important. It is the new technique for the
1990s.

REFERENCES

Bettger, F., *How I Raised Myself from Failure to Success in Selling*, Prentice-Hall, New Jersey, 1949.

Cattell, R.B., *The Scientific Analysis of Personality*, Penguin Books, Middlesex, 1968.

Chandler & Macleod Consultants Pty Ltd, *Human Relations Manual*, Sydney, 1972.

Denny, R., *Selling to Win*, Kogan Page, London, 1989.

Eysenck, H.J. & Wilson, G., *Know Your Own Personality*, Maurice Temple Smith, London, 1975.

Forbes Ley, D., *The Best Seller*, Kogan Page, London, 1988.

Harvey, C., *Your Pursuit of Profit*, Kogan Page, London, 1988.

Hopkins, T., *How to Master the Art of Selling*, Champion Press, Arizona, 1980.

Humm, D.G., 'Personality and Adjustment', *The Journal of Psychology*, 13, 1942, New York, pp. 109–34.

Humm, D.G.E. and Wadsworth, G.W. Jr., 'The Humm-Wadsworth Temperament Scale', *American Journal of Psychiatry*, 1, 1935, New York, pp. 163–200.

Moine, D.J. and Herd, J.H., *Modern Persuasion Strategies, The Hidden Advantage in Selling*, Prentice-Hall, New Jersey, 1984.

Rosanoff, A.J., *Manual of Psychiatry* (6th edn), Wiley, New York, 1938.

Salerno, S., *TNS The Newest Profession*, William Morrow, New York, 1985.

Schiffman, S., *The 25 Most Common Sales Mistakes ... and How to Avoid Them*, Kogan Page, London, 1991.

Stevenson, K., *Go Selling - A Sales Anthology*, Unlimited Marketing, Sydney, 1968.

Tirbutt, E., *How to Increase Sales Without Leaving Your Desk*, Kogan Page, London, 1988.

APPENDIX:
Personality Component Summaries

The Ditherer

Dominant Desire:	Desire for security
Identifying Clues:	
Talk:	Hypochondriac, gloomy outlook
Organisation:	Insurance
Position:	Administration
Dress:	Earth colours, brown cardigans
Office:	Filled with files, family photos
Gambit:	Early or late, never at the agreed time
Sales Strategies:	Security, long sale, repeated yes, ask for criticism of present supplier, instant replay, meet on Monday mornings
Common Objections:	Loyalty to existing supplier, I do not like your company, Your proposition is not good enough
Best Close:	Assume the sale

The Mover

Dominant Desire	Desire to communicate
Identifying Clues:	
Talk:	Lively, enthusiastic, smiles
Organisation:	Retailer, fast foods
Position:	Sales
Dress:	Tousled, shirtsleeves, yellow
Office:	Messy and chaotic
Gambit:	Late/informal
Sales Strategies:	Smile, repeated yes, emphasise group benefits, take prospect to meet other members of your organisation
Common Objections:	So friendly they rarely offer objections
Best Close:	Ask for the order again and again — Movers are not offended by repeated requests

The Engineer

Dominant Desire:	Desire to complete projects
Identifying Clues:	
Talk:	Monotonic
Organisation:	Consultant
Position:	Project manager
Dress:	Pens in pocket
Office:	Project plan, white boards, crammed bookcase
Gambit:	On time/informal
Sales Strategies:	Technical, overwhelm with manuals, action-feeling words, dummy runs, timetables and objectives, enjoys a drink
Common Objections:	I will not make a decision now, your proposition is not good enough, bad past experience with your company
Best Close:	Physical Action (Try the product out for three weeks)

The Hustler

Dominant Desire:	Desire for material success
Identifying Clues:	
Talk:	Money
Organisation:	Wholesalers, agents and brokers
Position:	Sales
Dress:	Flashy, red ties, lots of gold accessories
Office:	Glitzy, oranges and reds
Gambit:	On time/informal
Sales Strategies:	Top restaurants, discounts, golf with your MD, name drop, must offer a special deal only 'winners' get
Common Objections:	Price, I do not like you, Your proposition is not good enough
Best Close:	Inducement (Buy now and get 10% off the price)

The Politician

Dominant Desire:	Desire to win
Identifying Clues:	
Talk:	Opinionated, self-referring
Organisation:	Large and status driven
Position:	Manager
Dress:	Conventional (blue pinstripe)
Office:	Degrees, big office, important position
Gambit:	Late/formal
Sales Strategies:	Reference sell with large organisations, close on minor points, ask for help, auditory words, appeal to status
Common Objections:	Bad past experience with your company, I do not like you, I do not like your company
Best Close:	Subordinate question; e.g. Do you want it in pink or blue?

The Normal

Dominant Desire:	Desire for social approval
Identifying Clues:	
Talk:	Logical, rational, seeks group approval
Organisation:	Professional, e.g. accountant
Position:	Administration
Dress:	Conservative, old school tie, black, white and grey.
Office:	Neat and tidy
Gambit:	On time/formal
Sales Strategies:	Business cards, brochures, references, logic
Common Objections:	Price, I do not like your company, Your proposition is not good enough
Best Close:	Narrative, recapitulate the major benefits

The Artist

Dominant Desire:	Desire to be creative
Identifying Clues:	
Talk:	Bashful
Organisation:	Design
Position:	Creative executive
Dress:	Creative, unusual colours and prints
Office:	Original oil paintings and desk pieces
Gambit:	On time/formal
Sales Strategies:	Visual words, appeal to imagination, avoid eye contact, very soft sell, long sell, instant replay (Have ever bought something like this before? Tell me about it.)
Common Objections:	Loyalty to existing supplier, I do not like you, I will not make a decision now
Best Close:	Impending event (buy before prices go up)

INDEX